ALSO BY PETER MENDELSUND

Cover

PETER MENDELSUND is the associate art director of Alfred A. Knopf, the art director of Pantheon Books, and a recovering classical pianist. His designs have been described by *The Wall Street Journal* as being "the most instantly recognizable and iconic book covers in contemporary fiction." He lives in New York.

What

We

See

When

We

Read

WHAT WE SEE
WHEN WE READ

A PHENOMENOLOGY

WITH ILLUSTRATIONS

PETER
MENDELSUND

VINTAGE BOOKS   A DIVISION OF RANDOM HOUSE LLC   NEW YORK

FIRST VINTAGE BOOKS EDITION, AUGUST 2014

Copyright © 2014 by Peter Mendelsund

All rights reserved. Published in the United States by Vintage Books,
a division of Random House LLC, New York,
a Penguin Random House company.

Vintage and colophon are registered trademarks of
Random House LLC.

The Cataloging-in-Publication Data is on file at
the Library of Congress.

Vintage Trade Paperback ISBN: 978-0-8041-7163-2
eBook ISBN: 978-0-8041-7164-9

Book design by Peter Mendelsund
Cover design by Peter Mendelsund

www.vintagebooks.com

Printed in the United States of America

10   9   8   7   6   5   4   3   2

For my daughters

"A proposition is a picture of reality.
A proposition is a model of reality as we imagine it."
—Ludwig Wittgenstein,
Tractatus Logico-Philosophicus

"I don't think I shall ever forget my first sight of Hercule
Poirot. Of course, I got used to him later on, but to begin
with it was a shock . . . I don't know what I'd imagined . . .
Of course, I knew he was a foreigner, but I hadn't expected
him to be quite as foreign as he was, if you know what I
mean. When you saw him you just wanted to laugh! He
was like something on the stage or at the pictures."
—Agatha Christie,
Murder in Mesopotamia

"Writing . . . is but a different name for conversation. As
no one, who knows what he is about in good company,
would venture to *talk all*; so no author, who understands
the just boundaries of decorum and good breeding, would
presume to *think all*: The truest respect which you can
pay to the reader's understanding is to halve this matter
amicably, and leave him something to imagine, in his
turn, as well as yourself."
—Laurence Sterne,
*The Life and Opinions of
Tristram Shandy, Gentleman*

"The fancy cannot cheat so well as she is famed to do,
deceiving elf."
—John Keats,
"Ode to a Nightingale"

PICTURING

"PICTURING"

I could begin with Lily Briscoe.

Lily Briscoe—"With her little Chinese eyes and her puckered-up face . . ."—is a principal character in Virginia Woolf's novel *To the Lighthouse*. Lily is a painter. She is painting a picture throughout the course of the narrative—a painting of Mrs. Ramsay sitting by the window reading to her son James. Lily has set up her easel outside on the lawns and she paints while various players flit and charge about the property.

She is nervous about being interrupted, about someone breaking her concentration while she is engaged in this delicate act. The idea that someone would interrogate her about the painting is intolerable.

But kind, acceptable Mr. Bankes wanders up, examines her work, and asks what she wished to indicate "by the triangular purple shape, 'just there.'" (It is meant to be Mrs. Ramsay and her son, though "no one could tell it for a human shape.")

> *Mother and child then—objects of universal veneration, and in this case the mother was famous for her beauty—might be reduced, he pondered, to a purple shadow . . .*

Mother and child: reduced.

***

We never see this picture (the picture Lily paints in Virginia Woolf's novel). We are only told about it.

Lily is painting the scene that we, as readers, are being asked to imagine. (We are asked to imagine both: the scene and its painted likeness.)

***

This might be a good place to begin: with the picture that Lily paints; with its shapes, smudges, and shadows. The painting is Lily's reading of the tableau in front of her.

I cannot see the scene that Lily is attempting to capture.

I cannot see Lily herself. She is, in my mind, a scarcely perceptible hieroglyph.

The scene and its occupants are blurred.

Strangely, the painting seems more . . . vivid.

***

FICTIONS

"A world of disorderly notions, picked out of his books,
crowded into his imagination."—*Don Quixote in his library*

What do we see when we read?

(Other than words on a page.)

What do we picture in our minds?

There is a story called "Reading."

We all know this story.

It is a story of pictures, and of *picturing*.

The story of reading is a remembered story. When we read, we are immersed. And the more we are immersed, the less we are able, in the moment, to bring our analytic minds to bear upon the experience in which we are absorbed. Thus, when we discuss the feeling of reading we are really talking about the memory of having read.*

And this memory of reading is a false memory.

*William James describes the impossible attempt to introspectively examine our own consciousness as "trying to turn up the gas quickly enough to see how the darkness looks."

When we remember the
experience of reading a book,
we imagine a continuous
unfolding of images.

For instance, I remember reading Leo Tolstoy's *Anna Karenina*:

"I saw Anna; I saw Anna's house . . ."

1

2

We imagine that the experience of reading
is like that of watching a film.

WE SEE

VE READ!

tures
RESERVED

But this is not what actually happens—this is
neither what reading is, nor what reading *is like*

If I said to you, "Describe Anna Karenina," perhaps you'd mention her beauty. If you were reading closely you'd mention her "thick lashes," her weight, or maybe even her little downy mustache (yes—it's there). Mathew Arnold remarks upon "Anna's shoulders, and masses of hair, and half-shut eyes . . ."

But what does Anna Karenina look like? You may feel intimately acquainted with a character (people like to say, of a brilliantly described character, "it's like I know her"), but this doesn't mean you are actually picturing a person. Nothing so fixed—nothing so choate.

***

Anna Karenina, rendered by police composite-sketch software based on the descriptions in Tolstoy's text. (I always imagined her hair as being more tightly curled, and blacker . . .)

Most authors (wittingly, unwittingly) provide their fictional characters with more behavior than physical description. Even if an author excels at physical description, we are left with shambling concoctions of stray body parts and random detail (authors can't tell us *everything*). We fill in gaps. We shade them in. We gloss over them. We elide. Anna: her hair, her weight—these are facets only, and do not make up a true image of a person. They make up a body type, a hair color . . . *What does Anna look like?* We don't know—our mental sketches of characters are worse than police composites.

Visualizing seems to require will . . .

. . . though at times it may also seem as though an image of a sort appears to us unbidden.

(It is tenuous, and withdraws shyly upon scrutiny.)

I canvass readers. I ask them if they can clearly imagine their favorite characters. To these readers, a beloved character is, to borrow William Shakespeare's phrase, "bodied forth."

These readers contend that the success of a work of fiction hinges on the putative authenticity of the characters. Some readers go further and suggest that the only way they can enjoy a novel is if the main characters are easily visible:

"Can you picture, in your mind, what Anna Karenina looks like?" I ask.

> *"Yes,"* they say, *"as if she were standing here in front of me."*
> "What does her nose look like?"
> *"I hadn't thought it out; but now that I think of it, she would be the kind of person who would have a nose like . . ."*
> "But wait—how did you picture her before I asked? Noseless?"
> *"Well . . ."*
> "Does she have a heavy brow? Bangs? Where does she hold her weight? Does she slouch? Does she have laugh lines?"

(Only a very tedious writer would tell you this much about a character.*)

***

*Though Tolstoy never tires of mentioning Anna's *slender hands*. What does this emblematic description signify for Tolstoy?

Some readers swear they can picture these characters perfectly, but only while they are reading. I doubt this, but I wonder now if our images of characters are vague because our visual memories are vague in general.

**

A thought experiment: Picture your mother. Now picture your favorite literary character. (Or: Picture your home. Then picture Howards End.) The difference between your mother's afterimage and that of a literary character you love is that the more you concentrate, the more your mother might come into focus. A character will not reveal herself so easily. (The closer you look, the farther away she gets.)

(Actually, this is a relief. When I impose a face on a fictional character, the effect isn't one of recognition, but dissonance. I end up imagining someone I know.* And then I think: *That isn't Anna!*)

*I recently had the experience while reading a novel wherein I thought I had clearly "seen" a character, a society woman with "widely spaced eyes." When I subsequently scrutinized my imagination, I discovered that what I had been imagining was the face of one of my coworkers, grafted onto the body of an elderly friend of my grandmother's. When brought *into focus*, this was not a pleasant sight.

Often, when I ask someone to describe the physical appearance of a key character from their favorite book they will tell me how this character moves through space. (Much of what takes place in fiction is choreographic.)

One reader told me Benjy Compson from William Faulkner's *The Sound and the Fury* was "lumbering, uncoordinated . . ."

But what does he *look* like?

***

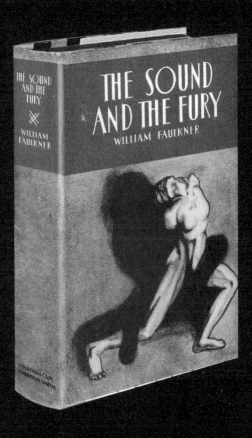

Literary characters are physically vague—they have only a few features, and these features hardly seem to matter—or, rather, these features matter only in that they help to refine a character's *meaning*. Character description is a kind of circumscription. A character's features help to delineate their boundaries—but these features don't help us truly picture a person.*

***

It is precisely what the text does not elucidate that becomes an invitation to our imaginations. So I ask myself: Is it that we imagine the most, or the most vividly, when an author is at his most elliptical or withholding?

(In music, notes and chords define ideas, but so do *rests*.)

*Or is it that *comprehensiveness* is not an important factor in the identification of anything?

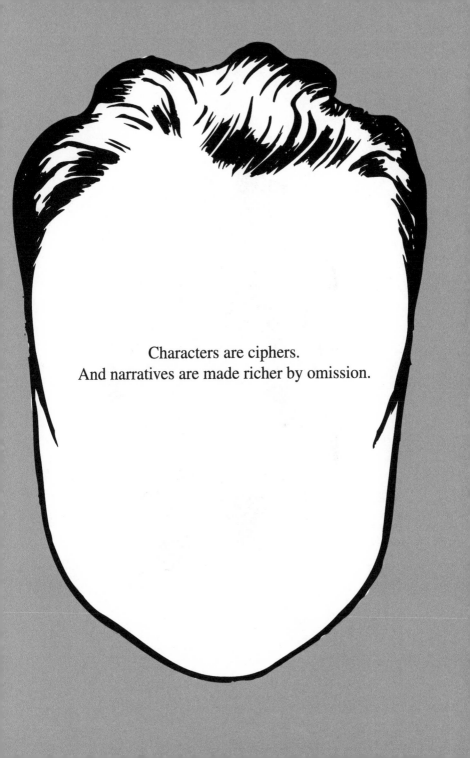

Characters are ciphers.
And narratives are made richer by omission.

William Gass, on Mr. Cashmore from Henry James's
The Awkward Age:

> *We can imagine any number of other sentences about*
> *Mr. Cashmore added . . . now the question is: what is*
> *Mr. Cashmore? Here is the answer I shall give: Mr.*
> *Cashmore is (1) a noise, (2) a proper name, (3) a com-*
> *plex system of ideas, (4) a controlling perception, (5)*
> *an instrument of verbal organization, (6) a pretended*
> *mode of referring, and (7) a source of verbal energy.*

The same could be said of any character—of Nanda,
from the same book, or of Anna Karenina. Of course—
isn't the fact that Anna is ineluctably drawn to Vronsky
(and feels trapped in her marriage) more significant
than the mere morphological fact of her being, say,
"full-figured"?

It is how characters behave, in relation to everyone
and everything in their fictional, delineated world, that
ultimately matters. ("Lumbering, uncoordinated . . .")

Though we may think of characters as visible, they are more like a set of rules that determines a particular outcome. A character's physical attributes may be ornamental, but their features can also contribute to their meaning.

(What is the difference between seeing and understanding?)

$$(A \bullet K \bullet V \bullet M) \supset$$

$$[(a \cup v) \vdash T]$$

A = Anna is young and pretty (is in possession of "slender hands"; is pleasingly plump; is pale and blushing; has masses of dark curly hair; etc.)

K = Karenin is old and ugly.

V = Vronsky is young and handsome.

M = Mores: i.e., the condemnation of extramarital affairs (by women) in nineteenth-century Russia

T = Anna will be killed by a train.

"a," "k," & "v" = Anna, Karenin, & Vronsky

Take Karenin's ears . . .

(Karenin is the cuckolded husband of Anna Karenina.)

Are his ears large or small?

> *At Petersburg, so soon as the train stopped and she got out, the first person that attracted her attention was her husband. 'Oh, mercy! Why do his ears look like that?' she thought, looking at his frigid and imposing figure, and especially the ears that struck her at the moment as propping up the brim of his round hat . . .*

Karenin's ears grow in proportion to his wife's disaffection with him. In this way, these ears tell us nothing about how Karenin looks, and a great deal about how Anna feels.

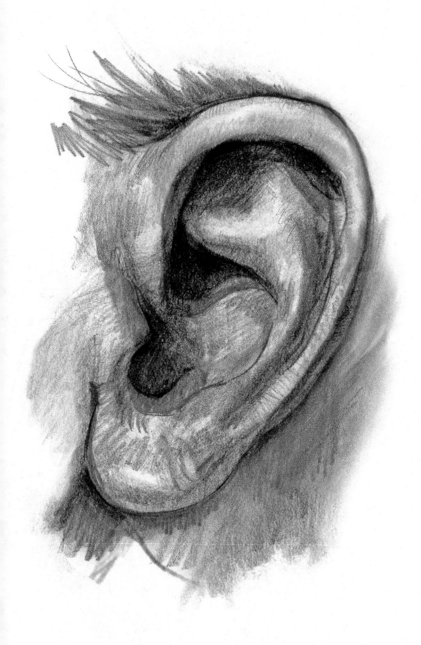

"Call me . . .

Ishmael."

What happens when you read the first line of Herman Melville's *Moby-Dick*?

You are being addressed, but by whom? Chances are you *hear* the line (in your mind's ear) before you picture the speaker. I can hear Ishmael's words more clearly than I can see his face. (Audition requires different neurological processes than vision, or smell. And I would suggest that we *hear* more than we see while we are reading.)

If you did manage to summon an image of Ishmael, what did you come up with? A seafaring man of some sort? (Is this a picture or a category?) Do you picture Richard Basehart, the actor in the John Huston adaptation?

(One should watch a film adaptation of a favorite book only after considering, *very carefully*, the fact that the casting of the film may very well become the permanent casting of the book in one's mind. This is a *very real hazard*.)

What color is *your* Ishmael's hair? Is it curly or straight? Is he taller than you? If you don't picture him clearly, do you merely set aside a chit, a placeholder that says, "Protagonist, narrator—first person"? Maybe this is enough. Ishmael probably evokes a feeling in you—but this is not the same as seeing him.

Maybe Melville had a specific image in mind for his Ishmael. Maybe Ishmael looked like someone he knew from his years at sea. But Melville's image is not ours. And no matter how well illustrated Ishmael may or may not be (I can't remember if Melville describes Ishmael's physical attributes, and I've read the book three times), chances are we will have to constantly revise our image of him as the book progresses. We are ever reviewing and reconsidering our mental portraits of characters in novels: amending them, backtracking to check on them, updating them when new information arises . . .

What kind of face you assign to Ishmael might depend upon what mood you are in on a particular day. Ishmael might look as different from one chapter to the next as, say, Tashtego does from Stubb.

Tashtego

Queequeg

Dagoo

Sometimes, in a *play*, several actors perform a single role. In these instances, the cognitive dissonance aroused by multiple actors is evident to the theatrical audience. But after reading a novel, we think back on its characters as if they were played by single actors. (In a narrative, multiplicity of "character" is read as psychological complexity.)

***

A question: Emma Bovary's eye color (famously) changes during the course of Gustave Flaubert's novel *Madame Bovary.* Blue, brown, deep black . . . Does this matter?

It doesn't appear to.

**

"I feel sorry for novelists when they have to mention women's eyes: there's so little choice . . . Her eyes are blue: innocence and honesty. Her eyes are black: passion and depth. Her eyes are green: wildness and jealousy. Her eyes are brown: reliability and common sense. Her eyes are violet: the novel is by Raymond Chandler."

—Julian Barnes, *Flaubert's Parrot*

Another question: As a character develops throughout the course of a novel, does the way this character "looks" to you (their appearance) change . . . as a result of their inner development? (A real person may become more beautiful to us once we are better acquainted with their nature—and in these cases our increased affection isn't due to some closer physical observation.)

Are characters complete as soon as they are introduced? Perhaps they are complete, but just *out of order*; the way a puzzle might be.

***

To the Lighthouse is a novel that is exemplary for, among other merits, its close descriptions of sensory and psychological experience. The raw material of the book isn't as much character, place, and plot as it is sense data.

The book opens like this:

"'Yes, of course, if it's fine tomorrow,' said Mrs. Ramsay."

I imagine these words echoing in a void. Who is Mrs. Ramsay? *Where* is she? She is speaking to someone. Two faceless people in a void—inchoate and unconstituted.

As we read on, Mrs. Ramsay becomes a collage, composed of clippings, like the ones in her son James's book.

***

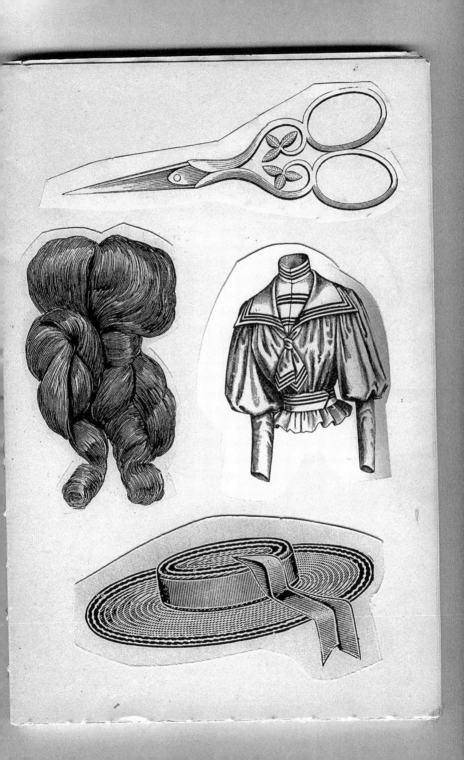

Mrs. Ramsay is speaking to her son, we are told. Is she, perhaps, seventy—and he fifty? No, we learn that he is only six. Revisions are made. And so on. If fiction were linear we would learn to wait, in order to picture. But we don't wait. We begin imaging right out of the gate, immediately upon beginning a book.

When we *remember* reading books, we don't remember having made these constant little adjustments.

Once again: We simply remember it as if we had watched the movie . . .

OPENINGS

When I read, I withdraw from the phenomenal world. I turn my attention "inward." Paradoxically, I turn outward toward the book I am holding, and, as if the book were a mirror, I feel as though I am *looking* inward. (This idea of a mirror is an analogy for the act of reading. And I can imagine other analogies as well: For instance, I can imagine reading is like withdrawing to a cloister behind my eyes—an open court, hemmed by a covered path; a fountain, a tree—a place of contemplation. But this is not what I see when I read. I don't see a cloister, or a mirror. What I see when I'm reading is not the act of reading itself, nor do I see analogies for the act of reading.)

When I read, my retirement from the phenomenal world is undertaken too quickly to notice. The world in front of me and the world "inside" me are not merely adjacent, but overlapping; superimposed. A book feels like the intersection of these two domains—or like a conduit; a bridge; a passage between them.

When my eyes are closed, the seen (the aurora borealis of my inner lids) and the imagined (say, an image of Anna Karenina) are never more than a volitional flick away from each other. Reading is like this closed-eye world—and reading takes place behind lids of a sort. An open book acts as a blind—its boards and pages shut out the world's clamorous stimuli and encourage the imagination.

Unc intentiore nobis opus est animo multo ch erat i supior solutione questionu z explicatone libron. De theologia quippe cp naturale vocat: no cuz quibuslibet hoibus: no eni fabulosa e vel ciuilis: hoc est vel theatrica vel vrbana: quaru altera iactitat deor crimina: altera indicat eor desideria crimiosiora: ac p h malignor pot demonu ...ci cu philosophis...

ab eis
...dum post
...rte. In hoc li
bro incipit dispu
tare cu phis con
tra theologia na
turalem: volens
ostendere cp illi q
ab eisvocant vij
vel demones: no
sunt colendi pro
ter aliqo bonu
...ture: z vi
...pars in
...mo

tum: qui ei
tem z humana cu
sentiat: no tn sufficere v...
incomutabilis dei cultu
ad vita adipiscenda etia
post morte beata: sed ab il
lo sane mitos vno oditos
atq institutos ob ea cau
sam colendos putant. Hi
etiam iam varronis opini
one veritatis ppinquitate
trascendut. Siquidez ille
tota theologia naturalem
vscp ad mundum istum vl
eius animam extedere po
tuit: isti vero sup omn
anime natura ...
qui no sols...

a v Ebo
tone ee. In b
incipit tractat
libri: in quo beat
gustin incipit age
de editionib
nis z pbor
dam alio
ctrinis

The openings of *To the Lighthouse* and *Moby-Dick* are confusing for the reader—we haven't yet been given sufficient information to begin processing the narrative and its imagery.

But we are used to such confusion. All books open in doubt and dislocation.

When you first open a book, you enter a liminal space. You are neither in this world, the world wherein you hold a book (say, *this* book), nor in that world (the metaphysical space the words point toward). To some extent this polydimensionality describes the feeling of reading in general—one is in

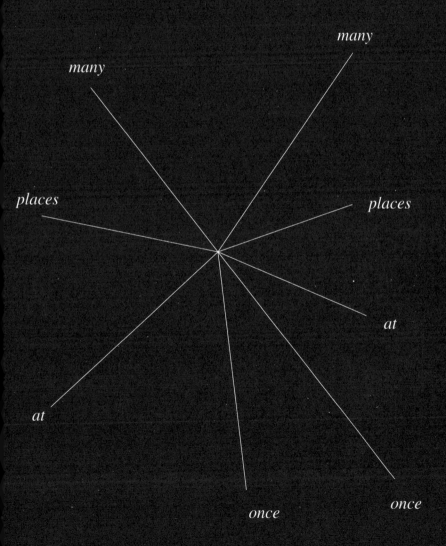

Italo Calvino describes this intermediacy . . .

The novel begins in a railway station, a locomotive huffs, steam from a piston covers the opening of the chapter, a cloud of smoke hides part of the first paragraph.

If on a
winter's
night
a traveler

The novel begins in a railway station, a locomotive huffs,
steam from a piston covers the opening of the chapter, a
cloud of smoke hides part of the first paragraph. In the
odor of the station there is a passing whiff of station café
odor. There is someone looking through the befogged
glass, he opens the glass door of the bar, everything is
misty, inside, too, as if seen by nearsighted eyes, or eyes
irritated by coal dust. The pages of the book are clouded
like the windows of an old train, the cloud of smoke rests
on the sentence. It is a rainy evening; the man enters the
bar; he unbuttons his damp overcoat; a cloud of steam
enfolds him; a whistle dies away along tracks that are
glistening with rain, as far as the eye can see.

A whistling sound, like a locomotive's, and a cloud of
steam rise from the coffee machine that the old counter-
man puts under pressure, as if he were sending up a signal, or at least so it seems from the series of sentences in
the second ... in which the players at the table
lose the ... ds against their chests and turn
ward th ... with a triple twist of their necks,

Bleak House als◌

LONDON. . . . As much mud in the streets as if the waters h
derful to meet a Megalosaurus, forty feet long or so, waddlin
chimney-pots, making a soft black drizzle, with flakes of so
imagine, for the death of the sun. Dogs, undistinguishably in
sengers, jostling one another's umbrellas in a gene
thousands of other foot passengers have been slip
the crust upon crust of mud, sticking at tho

Fog everywhere. Fog up the river, where it flo
tiers of shipping and the waterside pollution
creeping into the cabooses of collier-brigs; fog in
gunwales of barges and small boats. Fog in the
wards; fog in the stem and bowl of the afternoon
fingers of his shivering little 'prentice b
with fog all round them, as if the

Gas looming through
bandman and plough
unwilling look

The raw afternoon
appropriate ornament
at the very heart of the fog

Bleak House opens in fog—and this fog is a component part of the world Charles Dickens has written into being.

The fog is also a reference to the "actual" fog of London.

This fog is also a metaphor for the English chancery court system.

I just used this same fog as a visual metaphor for the openings of books in general.

The only one of these fogs that is completely indecipherable to me is the *visual effect*, in fiction, of *fog*.

TIME

I read a book aloud to my daughter. I read this passage to her:

"Then he heard a scream . . . it came from nearby . . ."

When I performed that scream for my daughter, it was in an uninflected, neutral voice—not because I can't act (although I can't), but because I didn't yet know which character was screaming. When I learned, farther down the page, who the screaming character was, my daughter made me go back and read the passage again—this time with a high, girlish voice appropriate to that particular character . . .

This is the process through which we visualize characters. We start thinking of them one way—and then lo, fifty pages later, we find out they are different from our mental placeholder in some crucial way, and we readjust.

***

James Joyce's *Ulysses* opens like so:

STATELY, PLUMP

Buck Mulligan came from the stairhead, bearing a bowl of lather on which a mirror and a razor lay crossed. A yellow dressinggown, ungirdled, was sustained gently behind him on the mild morning air. He held the bowl aloft and intoned:

—*Introibo ad altare Dei.*

Halted, he peered down the dark winding stairs and called up coarsely:

—Come up, Kinch! Come up, you fearful jesuit!

Solemnly he came forward and mounted the round gunrest. He faced about and blessed gravely thrice the tower, the surrounding country and the awaking mountains. Then, catching sight of Stephen Dedalus, he bent towards him and made rapid crosses in the air, gurgling in his throat and shaking his head. Stephen Dedalus, displeased and sleepy, leaned his arms on the top of the staircase and looked coldly at the shaking gurgling face that blessed him, equine in its length, and at the light untonsured hair, grained and hued like pale oak.

Buck Mulligan peeped an instant under the mirror and then covered the bowl smartly.

—Back to barracks, he said sternly.

He added in a preacher's tone:

—For this, O dearly beloved, is the genuine Christine: body and soul and blood and ouns. Slow music, please. Shut your eyes, gents. One moment. A little trouble about those white corpuscles. Silence, all.

He peered sideways up and gave a long slow whistle of call, then paused awhile in rapt attention, his even white teeth glistening here and there with gold points. Chrysostomos. Two strong shrill whistles answered through the calm.

—Thanks, old chap, he cried briskly. That will do nicely. Switch off the current, will you?

He skipped off the gunrest and looked gravely at his watcher, gathering about his legs the loose folds of his gown. The plump shadowed face and sullen oval jowl recalled a prelate, patron of arts in the middle ages. A pleasant smile broke quietly over his lips.

—The mockery of it, he said gaily. Your absurd name, an ancient Greek!

He pointed his finger in friendly jest and went over to the parapet, laughing to himself. Stephen Dedalus stepped up, followed him wearily halfway and sat down on the edge of the gunrest, watching him still as he propped...

"Stately, plump Buck Mulligan . . ."

When Buck Mulligan appears, he comes at us adjectives first. His adjectives precede him.

A first reading of *Ulysses* might generate a series of static images in the reader's mind; each picture relating to Buck's descriptors, one by one, as they appear.

These adjectives are asynchronous; they may appear out of time.

Stately

Plump

BUCK

Mulligan

(or Mulligan)

The reading imagination reveals our own dispositions.
The book has drawn them out of us.

(Our dispositions are strange . . .)

"Mulligan"

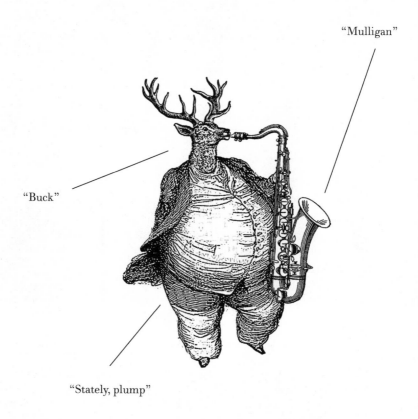

"Buck"

"Stately, plump"

The book might later eliminate these in favor of others.

But (of course) we do not apprehend words as we are
reading them . . .

one

at

a

time.

When we read, we take in whole eyefuls of words. We gulp them like water.

***

State
ly, plump Buck
Mulligan came
from the stairhead
bearing a bowl of father
on which a mirror and a
razor lay crossed. A yellow
dressinggown, ungirdled,
was sustained gently behind
him by the mild morning air.
He held the bowl aloft and
intoned:—*Introibo ad altare
Dei.* Halted, he peered down
the dark winding stairs and
called up coarsely:—Come
up, Kinch. Come up, you
fearful jesuit. Solemnly
he came forward and
mounted the round
gunrest. He faced
about and

blessed
gravely thrice
the tower, the sur-
rounding country and
the awaking mountains.
Then, catching sight of
Stephen Dedalus, he bent
idecrosses in the air gurgling
in his throat and shaking
his head. Stephen Dedalus,
displeased and sleepy, leaned
his arms on the top of the
staircase and looked coldly
at the shaking gurgling face
that blessed him, equine in
its length, and at the light
untonsured hair, grained
and hued like pale
oak. Buck Mulligan
peeped an instant
under the mir-
ror and

then
covered the
bowl smartly.—
Back to barracks!
he said sternly. He
added in a preacher's
tone:—For this, O dearly
beloved, is the genuine
Christine: body and soul
and blood and ouns. Slow
music, please. Shut your
eyes, gents. One moment.
A little trouble about those
white corpuscles. Silence,
all. He peered sideways up
and gave a long slow whistle
of call, then paused awhile in
rapt attention, his even white
teeth glistening here and there
with gold points. Chrysostomos.
Two strong shrill whistles
answered through the calm.—
Thanks, old chap, he cried
briskly. That will do nicely.
Switch off the current, will you?

about his
loose folds of his
gown. The plump
shadowed face and
sullen oval jowl recalled
a prelate, patron
of arts in the middle ages.
A pleasant smile
broke quietly over his
lips.—The mockery of it,
he said gaily. Your absurd
name, an ancient Greek.
He pointed his finger
in friendly jest and went over
to the parapet, laughing
to himself. Stephen Dedalus
stepped up, followed him
wearily halfway and sat
down on the edge of the
gunrest, watching him still
as he propped his mirror on
the parapet, dipped the brush
in and lathered cheeks
and neck.Buck Mulligan's
gay voice went on.—My
name is absurd too: Mal-
achi Mulligan, two
dactyls. But it has a
Hellenic ring, hasn't
it?...

A word's context matters. The significance of a word is contingent on the words that surround it. In this way, words are like musical notes. Imagine a single tone . . .

It is like a word out of context. You might consider such a single pitch as one might consider a noise (especially if the note is produced by, say, a car horn)—i.e., devoid of meaning.

Add another note and there is now some context with which to consider the first. A *chord* is now heard, even if one wasn't intended.

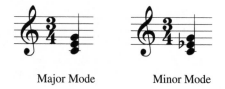

Major Mode   Minor Mode

Add a third note and meaning becomes further narrowed. Mood is changed utterly by virtue of context. So it is with words.

Context—not just semantic but narrative context—
accumulates only as one reads deeper and deeper into
a text.

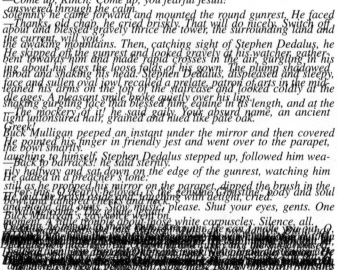

Stately, plump Buck Mulligan came from the stairhead, bearing a bowl
of lather on which a mirror and a razor lay crossed. A yellow dressinggown, ungirdled, was sustained gently behind him on the mild morning
air. He held the bowl aloft and intoned:
—Introibo ad altare Dei.
Halted, he peered down the dark winding stairs and called up coarsely:
—Come up, Kinch! Come up, you fearful jesuit!
Solemnly he came forward and mounted the round gunrest. He faced
about and blessed gravely thrice the tower, the surrounding land and
the awaking mountains. Then, catching sight of Stephen Dedalus, he
bent towards him and made rapid crosses in the air, gurgling in his
throat and shaking his head. Stephen Dedalus, displeased and sleepy,
leaned his arms on the top of the staircase and looked coldly at the
shaking gurgling face that blessed him, equine in its length, and at the
light untonsured hair, grained and hued like pale oak.
Buck Mulligan peeped an instant under the mirror and then covered
the bowl smartly.
—Back to barracks! he said sternly.
He added in a preacher's tone:
—For this, O dearly beloved, is the genuine Christine: body and soul
and blood and ouns. Slow music, please. Shut your eyes, gents. One
moment. A little trouble about those white corpuscles. Silence, all.

"WELL, NOW WE WILL FINISH TALKING AND GO TO HIS FUNERAL DINNER. DON'T BE PUT OU
PANCAKES—IT'S A VERY OLD CUSTOM AND THERE'S SOMETHING NICE IN THAT!" LAUG

"WELL, LET US GO! AND NOW WE GO HAND IN HAND."

"AND ALWAYS SO, ALL OUR LIVES HAND IN HAND! HURRAH FOR KARAMAZOV!" KOLYA CRIED O
OUSLY, AND ONCE MORE THE BOYS TOOK UP HIS EXCLAMATION: "HURRAH FOR KAR

FIN

Despite this fact—that our understanding of a narrative develops throughout the course of a story—I've noticed that the intensity of my imagination does not increase, as a result, toward the end of a book. The final pages of books are not full of spectacle, but rather, more *pregnant with significance.*

(I only want to underscore, again, the difference between seeing and understanding.)

***

In order to make sense of a book's words and phrases we must think ahead when we read—we must anticipate. This is how we readers contend with the cul-de-sacs, hiccups, gaps, and enjambments of our linear, written language.

We are picturing what we are told to see, but also we are picturing what we imagine we *will be told to see*, farther down the page. If a character rounds a corner, we predict what's around the bend (even if the author refuses to tell us).

We gulp words and phrases when we read quickly, but we also may choose to savor some texts, and roll them on our tongues.

(Does the speed at which we read affect the vividness of our imagination?)

***

Have you ever walked along the shoulder of a road upon which you normally drive? Details you hadn't seen at high speed are suddenly revealed. You learn that a road is really two different roads—one for pedestrians and another for passengers. These roads bear only a thin, cartographical relationship to each other. The experiences of these roads are utterly distinct.

If books were roads, some would be made for driving quickly—details are scant, and what details there are appear drab—but the velocity and torque of the narrative is exhilarating. Some books, if seen as roads, would be made for walking—the trajectory of the road mattering far less than the vistas these roads might afford. The best book for me: I drive through it quickly but am forced to stop on occasion, to pull over and marvel. These books are books meant to be reread. (The first time through, I can tear along, as fast as possible, and then later, I'll enjoy a leisurely stroll—so that I can see what I've missed.)

One type of novel

Another type of novel

I'm reading aloud to my daughter again. (I do this every night.)

I notice that I still read words from the end of a previous page after I've already turned to a new page.

(I've turned the page too

soon.)

Our eyes and our minds, as I've mentioned, read ahead.

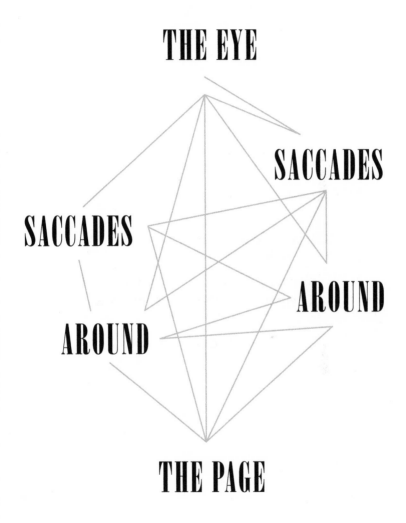

THE EYE

SACCADES

SACCADES

AROUND

AROUND

THE PAGE

I am picturing something from one part of the page as
I am gathering information from another.

At once (at a gulp) we readers:

1. Read a sentence . . .

2. Read several sentences ahead . . .

3. Maintain consciousness of the content of sentences we have already read . . .

4. Imagine events down the line.

The "eye-voice span" is the distance between where one's eyes are looking on a page and where, on the page, one's (inner) voice is reading.

Protention / Retention

past   now   future

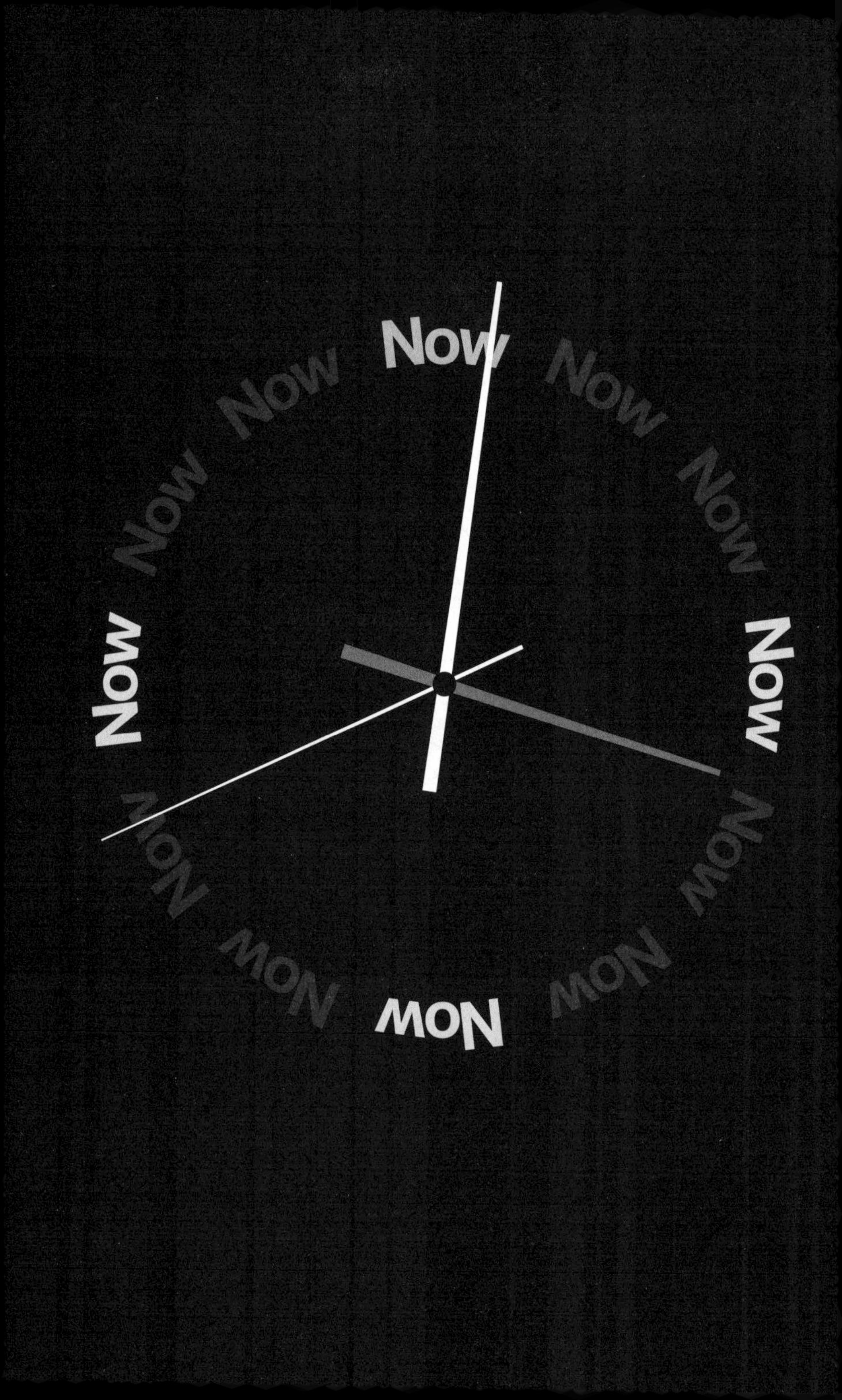
Now
Now
Now
Now
Now
Now
Now
Now
Now
Now
Now
Now

Reading is not a sequence of experienced "now"s . . .

Past, present, and future are interwoven in each conscious moment—and in the performative reading moment as well. Each fluid interval comprises an admixture of: the memory of things read (past), the experience of a consciousness "now" (present), and the anticipation of things to be read (future).

***

"I do not pass through a series of instances of now, the images of which I preserve and which, placed end to end, make a line. With the arrival of every moment, its predecessor undergoes a change: I still have it in hand and it is still there, but already it is sinking away below the level of presents; in order to retain it, I need to reach through a thin layer of time." —Maurice Merleau-Ponty

then

tnhoewn

now

Fictional characters do not appear to us *all at once*; they do not immediately materialize in our imaginations.

James Joyce's character Buck Mulligan is merely a cipher at the opening of *Ulysses*, but he becomes more nuanced over time—once we are witness to his interactions with the other actors in Joyce's novel. Through his dealings with the population of Dublin, Buck's other facets emerge. Slowly, he becomes complex.

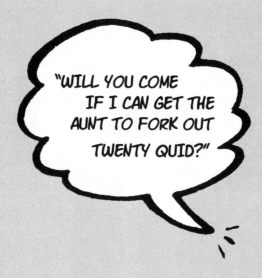

"WILL YOU COME IF I CAN GET THE AUNT TO FORK OUT TWENTY QUID?"

. . . he says to his roommate Stephen.

(He is a sponger.)

. . . he says of their absent third roommate, Haines.

(He is disloyal.)

(And so on.)

Buck's character, like the character of any literary figure, is an emergent phenomenon of action and interaction.

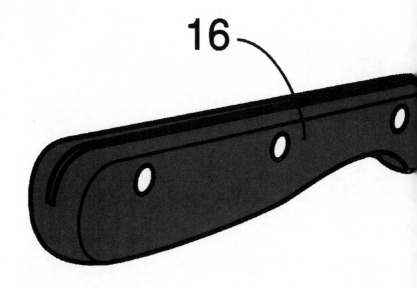

Action: Aristotle claimed that Self *is* an action, and that we discover something's nature through knowing its *telos* (its goals).

A knife becomes a knife through *cutting* . . .

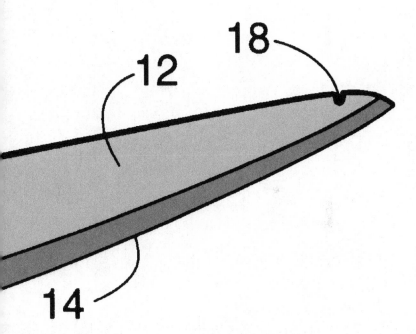

An actor friend tells me that, for him, the creation of a character is "more about the adverbs than the adjectives." I think what he means is that the (necessarily) insufficient facts about a character (provided by the author) don't matter as much as *what* a character does, and *how* that character does it. "Anyway," my friend continues, playwrights "don't supply that many adjectives."

(Are we better at imagining *actions* than we are at picturing *things*?)

***

"I like a lot of talk in a book and I don't like to have nobody tell me what the guy that's talking looks like. I want to figure out what he looks like from the way he talks . . . figure out what the guy's thinking from what he says. I like some description but not too much of that . . ."
—John Steinbeck, *Sweet Thursday*

What would an action look like if it didn't have a clear subject and object?

Can an image be composed solely of actions?

This is no more a possibility than that of building a sentence solely from verbs . . .

Opening sentences; only the verbs . . .

"Slandered arrested." —*The Trial*
"Came bearing crossed." —*Ulysses*
"See." —*The Sound and the Fury*
"Call." —*Moby-Dick*
"Are is." —*Anna Karenina*

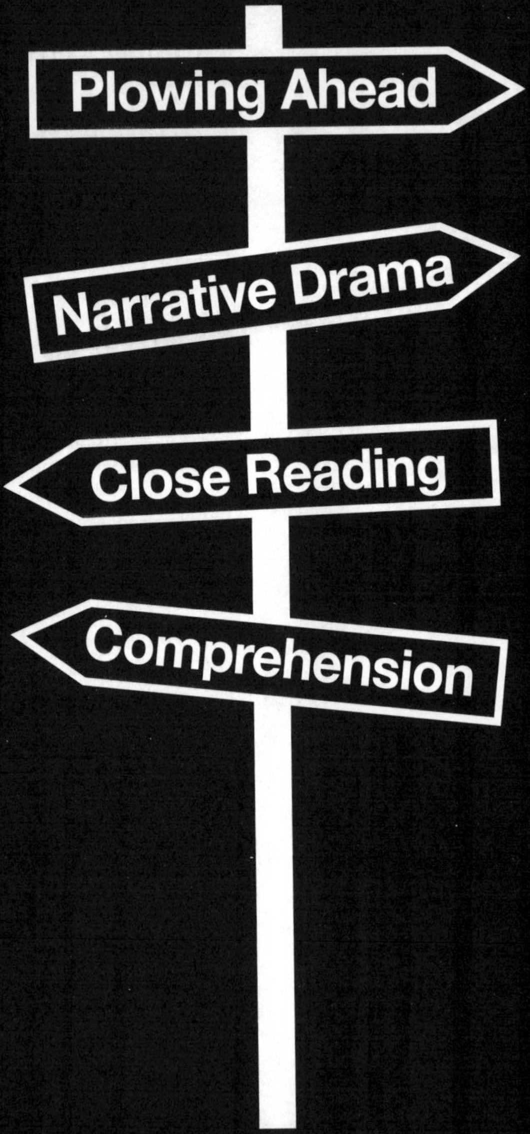
Plowing Ahead
Narrative Drama
Close Reading
Comprehension

Not long ago, I was reading a book when, suddenly, I jumped to attention—startled and embarrassed, like a tired driver drifting out of his lane. I had become conscious of the fact that I had no idea who a particular character I had been reading about *was*.

Had I not been reading carefully enough?

When a story reaches a confusing juncture—where there is a dislocation in time or space; when an unknown character appears in the text; if we begin to sense that we are ignorant of some seemingly crucial narrative fact—we are then faced with a dilemma: to go backwards and revisit earlier passages, or to press on.

(We make choices about how we choose to imagine, and we make choices about how we choose to read.)

In these cases, we may decide that we missed some key element, an event or explanation that came earlier in the book. And then we turn back the pages in an attempt to find the components of the story we've been missing.

Other times, however, it seems better to just continue reading, bracketing our ignorance and suspending resolution. We may wonder if it is the author's intention to reveal things slowly, and then we will be patient, as we tell ourselves a good reader should be. Or if we have indeed accidentally glossed over some crucial fact earlier in the book, we will decide that it is more important to continue, to remain in the moment, not to take ourselves out of the dramatic flow of the story. We decide that drama takes precedence over information. Especially if we deem that information unimportant.

It requires so little to plow ahead.

Characters can move through empty, undifferentiated spaces; rooms may contain unnamed, faceless, meaningless characters; seemingly purposeless subplots are endured as if read in a foreign language . . . we read on until we are, once again, oriented.

We can read without seeing, and we can also read without understanding. What happens to our imaginations when we have lost the narrative thread in a story, when we breeze past words we don't understand, when we read words without knowing to what they refer?

When I am reading a sentence in a book that references something unknown to me (as when I have inadvertently skipped a passage), I feel as though I am reading a syntactically correct but semantically meaningless "nonsense" sentence. The sentence *feels* meaningful—it has the *flavor* of meaning—and the structure of its grammar thrusts me forward through the sentence and on to the next, though in truth I understand (and picture) nothing.

How much of our reading takes place in such a suspension of meaning? How much time do we spend reading seemingly meaningful sentences without knowing their referrents? How much of our reading takes place in such a void—propelled by mere *syntax*?

All good books are, at heart, mysteries. (Authors with-hold information. This information may be revealed over time. This is one reason we bother to turn a book's pages.) A book may be a *literal* mystery (*Murder on the Orient Express*, *The Brothers Karamazov*) or a *metaphysical* mystery (*Moby-Dick*, *Doctor Faustus*) or a mystery of a purely architectonic kind—a chro-notopic mystery (*Emma*, *The Odyssey*).

The convict is Pip's benefactor

These mysteries are *narrative* mysteries—but books also defend their *pictorial secrets* . . .

* * *

"Call me Ishmael . . ."

This statement invites more questions than it answers. We desire that Ishmael's face be, like the identity of one of Agatha Christie's murderers:

Revealed!

GUILTY

GUILTY-ER

Writers of fiction tell us stories, and they also tell us how to read these stories. From a novel I assemble a series of rules—not only a methodology for reading (a suggested hermeneutics) but a manner of cognition, all of which carries me through the text (and sometimes lingers after a book ends). The author teaches me how to imagine, as well as *when* to imagine, and *how much*.

***

In a detective mystery I'm reading, a principal character is introduced as "sulky and heavy featured."

Does this description, "sulky and heavy featured," add to my sense of this character's appearance? The author does not seem to set down this picture for such a purpose. Instead of offering a portrayal, she offers up another kind of signification.

In the beginning of a classic detective novel we are introduced (as to a game board) to a bounded location containing limited players. The players correspond roughly to archetypes, which make them easier to remember, as well as easier to use for our mental mystery-solving calculations. Their names will be repeated often, as will a peculiar character trait. A seasoned reader of detective novels will recognize that character description is used here to signify guilt or innocence.

A mustache can be a clue, or even a motive. But more important, it can be a rank and purpose—and it tells the readers whether they are dealing with a pawn, a rook, a bishop, et cetera.

***

In the game that is "reading detective novels," the rules are codified—but also occasionally counterintuitive to the inexperienced. Such a character who is "sulky and heavy featured," or "dark," or "wildly unkempt," or who is in possession of a "shifting gaze" or a "vulpine mouth," will certainly, when all is said and done, be revealed to be innocent—a classic red herring. Occasionally, an author will be artless enough to genuinely telegraph a character's guilt through their appearance; and sometimes, an author will be so artful as to set up a false red herring: the shifty-eyed stranger *really is* the killer. In these cases, adjectives are feints, parries, moves, and countermoves.

***

(Character traits are also *instructions for use*.)

***

Schloss

Land Surveyor

127

In *Jane Eyre*, the tyrannical Mrs. Reed, a character introduced on page 1, is not fully (physically) described
until page 43. When we are finally granted a descriptive account of her, she appears like so:

> *Mrs. Reed might be at the time some six or seven
> and thirty; she was a woman of robust frame,
> square-shouldered and strong-limbed, not tall
> and, though stout, not obese; she had a somewhat
> large face, the under-jaw being much developed
> and very solid; her brow was low, her chin large
> and prominent, mouth and nose sufficiently reg-
> ular; under her light eyebrows glimmered an eye
> devoid of ruth; her skin was dark and opaque, her
> hair nearly flaxen; her constitution was sound as
> a bell . . . she dressed well and had a presence and
> port calculated to set off handsome attire.*

Why does Charlotte Brontë wait so long to illustrate
this critical figure? (And what have we been picturing
in the interim?)

Mrs. Reed has not been described until page 43 because she hasn't been fully looked at by the protagonist until that dramatic moment. Brontë is instead
attempting to describe Jane Eyre's experience of Mrs.
Reed. While Jane is Mrs. Reed's captive and tormented
ward, little Jane only takes in desperate glimpses of

a furious Mrs. Reed. Jane sees Mrs. Reed through clenched eyes—while Jane is in full flinch—so, for Jane, and thus for us, Mrs. Reed is revealed one scary bit at a time: her "formidable gray eye," her stout frame on the stair speeding two steps at a time.

When, finally, Jane confronts her oppressor and is able to, as it were, look her square in the eye, she is afforded a vista—a view of the whole—and can appraise it. In this case, the description is (almost) irrelevant; what matters is its *timing*.

As I mentioned, characters are mostly seen in action. We see them as we might see someone we are pursuing, a head above a crowd, a torso rounding corners, a foot there, a blurry leg here . . . in fiction, this amassing of discrete detail mirrors the way we assimilate people and settings in our daily lives.

Occasionally I'll meet someone I've heard a lot about, and I might think to myself, *You look nothing like what I imagined!*

I have the same feeling with characters in novels— when they are active *before* they are described.

(I had this same feeling with *Jane Eyre*'s Mrs. Reed.)

***

VIVIDNESS

In his *Lectures on Literature*, Vladimir Nabokov notes: "The first thing that we notice about the style of Dickens [in *Bleak House*] is his intensely sensuous imagery . . ."

When the sun shone through the clouds, making silvery pools in the dark sea . . .

Nabokov writes:

Let us pause: can we visualize that? Of course we can, and we do so with a greater thrill of recognition because in comparison to the conventional blue sea of literary tradition these silvery pools in the dark sea offer something that Dickens noted for the very first time with the innocent and sensuous eye of the true artist, saw and immediately put into words.

***

Another passage from Dickens:

> *The welcome light soon shines upon the wall, as Krook . . . comes up slowly with his green-eyed cat following at his heels.*

Nabokov, again:

> *All cats have green eyes—but notice how green these eyes are owing to the lighted candle . . .*

Nabokov seems to be making the point that the greater the specificity and context for an image, the more evocative it is.

(I'm not so sure.)

Specificity and context add to the meaning and perhaps to the expressiveness of an image, but do not seem to add to the *vividness* of my experience of an image— that is, all this authorial care, the author's observation and transcription of the world, does not help me to see. They help me to understand—but not to see. (At least, when I examine my responses to these types of descriptions, I do not perform any better in my attempts to envision the author's world.)

As a reader I am delighted by the candlelit eyes of the cat; their specificity. But my delight is not due to some *more vivid seeing*. My delight is my tribute to the author's having paid close attention to the world.

It is easy to confuse these two sensations.

***

Dickens:

*The person . . . receives his twopence . . . tosses
the money in the air, catches it over-handed, and
retires.*

Nabokov:

*This gesture, this one gesture, with its epithet
"over-handed"—a trifle—but the man is alive for-
ever in a good reader's mind.*

But is the character alive? Or is only his hand alive?

Dickens has conveyed something apparently true about the world, and the feeling of "truth" in this description derives from the description's specificity.

Writers closely observe the world and record their observations. When we remark that a novel is "finely observed," we are praising the writer's ability to bear witness. This bearing witness is composed of two acts: the author's initial observation in the real world, and then the translation of that observation into prose. The more "finely observed" the text, the better we readers recognize the thing or event in question. (Again— seeing and acknowledging are different activities.)

The author's specificity allows me, the reader, to acknowledge a dual achievement of my own: 1) I've scrutinized the world closely enough to notice such details (*silvery pools*) myself (I remember them), and 2) I am astute enough to recognize the author's art in calling out such a finely turned detail. I feel the thrill of recognition, but also the pleasure of self-satisfaction. (It's buried, but it's there.) Notice how Nabokov refers to a "good reader" in the previous passage?

***

A thing that is "captured" by an author is taken from its context in the real world, where this event or thing may exist in a state of flux. An author might notice a wave in the ocean (or a "silvery pool"), and merely by remarking upon this wave, the author stabilizes it. It is now removed from the indiscriminate mass of water that surrounds it. By taking this wave and holding it fast in language, it ceases to be fluid. It is now an *immobile* wave.

We examine Dickens's "silvery pools" through his *microscope*. Dickens has taken this event and placed it, contained, as if a solution on a slide, and enlarged it for us. What we are seeing is, at best, a distortion *through* that microscope's lens, and at worst, we are seeing only the microscope's lens itself. (To borrow a line of reasoning from the philosophy of science: What we are observing is not the thing itself, but the tools we have constructed to observe that thing.)

So when we praise "finely observed" prose, are we praising the evocative efficacy of the ideas, or the beauty of the equipment?

We imagine that it is both.

***

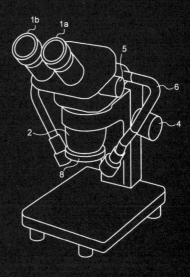

Descriptions that are more elaborate and read with greater attention and deliberation are not necessarily more vivid. They may be more explanatory, but they don't add up to a *gestalt*—a complete and simultaneous vision.

Read this long passage of Mark Twain's:

The first thing to see, looking away over the water, was a kind of dull line—that was the woods on t'other side—you couldn't make nothing else out; then a pale place in the sky; then more paleness, spreading around; then the river softened up, away off, and warn't black any more, but gray; . . . sometimes you could hear a sweep screaking; or jumbled up voices, it was so still, and sounds come so far; and by-and-by you could see a streak on the water which you know by the look of the streak that there's a snag there in the swift current which breaks on it and makes the streak look that way; and you see the mist curl up off of the water, and the east reddens up, and the river, and you make out a log cabin in the edge of the woods, away on the bank on t'other side of the river . . .

Did you see it all? I read this passage and I saw the dull line, and then the spreading paleness, and then I heard a screaking, and then voices, and then I saw the current . . .

How much detail an author supplies when describing the appearance of a character or a place will not improve a reader's mental pictures (it will not bring these pictures *into focus*); however, the level of detail provided by a writer does determine what *kind* of reading experience a reader might have. In other words, lists of attributes, in literature, may have *rhetorical* power, but lack combinatorial power.

We have the idea that a long descriptive passage *adds up* to something. For example, the city of Zenobia, from Calvino's *Invisible Cities*, is described in detail, therefore:

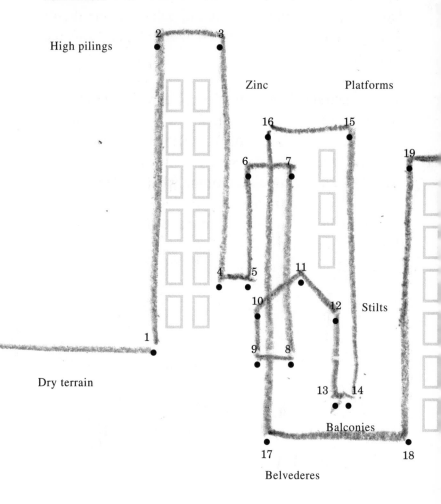

"For me, the main thing in a narrative is . . . the order of things . . . the pattern; the symmetry; the network of images deposited around it . . ."
—Italo Calvino, *Le Monde,* August 15, 1970

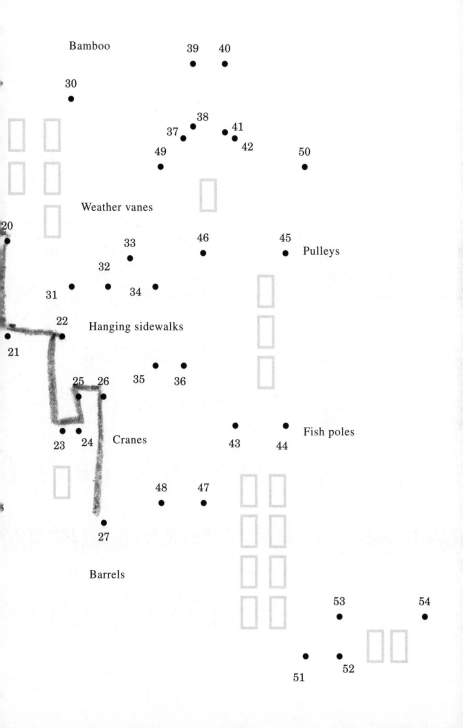

Bamboo

39 40

30

38
37 41
49 42 50

Weather vanes

33 46 45
32 Pulleys
31 34

22 Hanging sidewalks

21

35 36

25 26

23 24 Cranes 43 44 Fish poles

48 47

27

Barrels

53 54

51 52

But description is not additive. Twain's mist on the water does not carry over while I am seeing the log cabin. By the time I reach the words *log cabin*, I have forgotten about the mist entirely.*

Vision, however, is additive, and simultaneous.

* Jorge Luis Borges refers to the disparate elements listed in literary description as *disjecta membra*, which translates from the Latin as either "scattered (or *dismembered*) remains," or "broken pottery shards."

(We don't see a chair, and then hang around
in order to find out what color it is . . .)

Red

(Perhaps if I'm told the chair is red, and then the chair is mentioned again, I'll think: *Oh, the red chair . . .*)

Calvino's city of Zenobia is detailed. His city of
Chloe lacks detail. Here, the author allows—even
invites—fantasy.

1

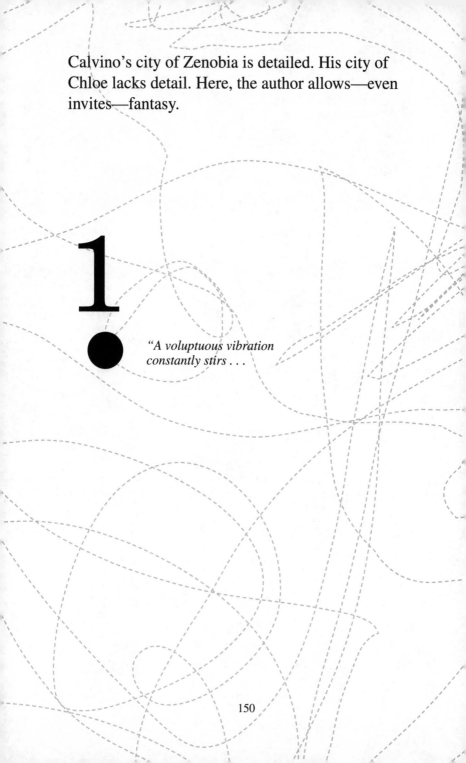

*"A voluptuous vibration
constantly stirs . . .*

In this case we experience the power of the unsaid.

X

" . . . The most chaste of cities . . ."

Invisible Cities again:

"Marco Polo describes a bridge, stone by stone. 'But which is the stone that supports the bridge?' Kublai Khan asks.

We may not see every image
(or every word) in a long description . . .

he bridge is not supported by one stone or another,' Marco Polo answers, 'but by the line of the arch that they form.'"

. . . but each word (or each image)
may be a *load-bearing* word (or image).

Maybe elaborate descriptions, like colorful descriptions, are misdirection. They seem to tell us something specific and meaningful (about a character, a setting, the world itself), but perhaps such description delights in inverse proportion to what it reveals.

More Colorful
Equals
Less Authentic

The writer Gilbert Sorrentino takes John Updike's *A Month of Sundays* to task:

> *When the aim is "vivid" writing, it seems that anything goes as long as the surface dances . . . The work buckles and falls apart time after time under the weight of this concatenation of images, often linked together by comparisons that work to conceal the reality they are supposedly revealing: ". . . newsletters and quarterlies that pour through a minister's letter slot like urine from a cow's vulva."*

Such writing is, Sorrentino tells us, "Shiny and meaningless."

The relationship between a mail slot and a cow's vulva is confusing. Two objects are compared in order to help focus our mind's eye, while in fact just the opposite happens—we focus only on the bolder (or in this case more grotesque) of the two images.

By contrast, Jean Giono writes: *"Look up there, Orion–Queen Anne's lace, a little bunch of stars."*

I see the flower, then I see the flowering of stars in the night sky. The flower itself doesn't appear in the night sky of my mind, but the flower determines how the stars are arrayed.*

(Giono could have written: "a little cluster of white stars." But this description doesn't *bloom* in quite the same way.)

* * *

---

* Giono's stars are clearer to me than Updike's mail slot. Maybe that is because Giono would like me to see his stars, whereas Updike would like me to see—what? His prose? Giono's flower and his stars are held in balance. One image assists the other.

PERFORMANCE

Once a reading of a book is under way, and we sink into the experience, a performance of a sort begins . . .

We perform a book—we perform a reading of a book. We perform a book, and we attend the performance.

(As readers, we are both the conductor and the orchestra, as well as the audience.)

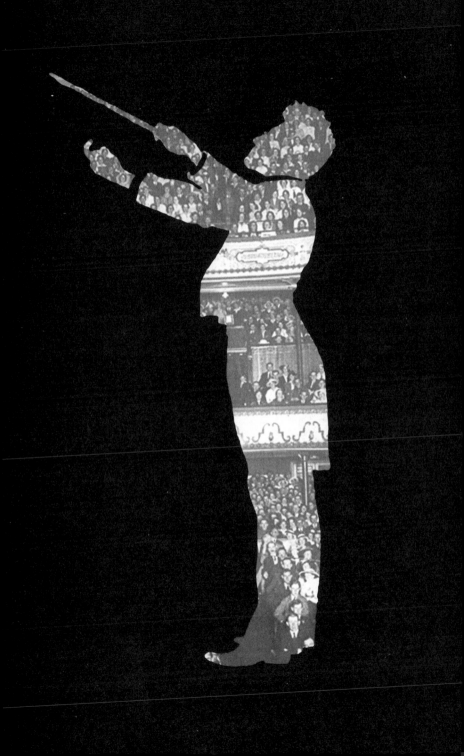

When we read, it is important that we believe we are seeing everything . . .

When I play the piano—as opposed to when I am listening to piano music—I don't hear my mistakes. My mind is too busy imagining an idealized performance to hear what is actually emanating from the instrument. In this sense, the performative aspects of playing the piano inhibit my ability to *hear.*

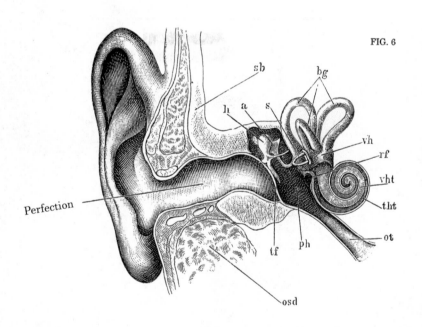

FIG. 6

sb
bg
h   a   s
vh
rf
vht
tht
Perfection
ot
tf   ph
osd

Similarly, when we read, we imagine that we see.

There are radical disjunctures in our readings . . .

We seem to know—if we are good readers—where in a text to find the information we need.

Though managing and executing these disjunctures is an integral part of the performative art of reading, when we remember reading a book, we gloss over this aspect of the experience.

To say fiction is linear is not to say we read in a straight line.

***

The eye jumps around

***

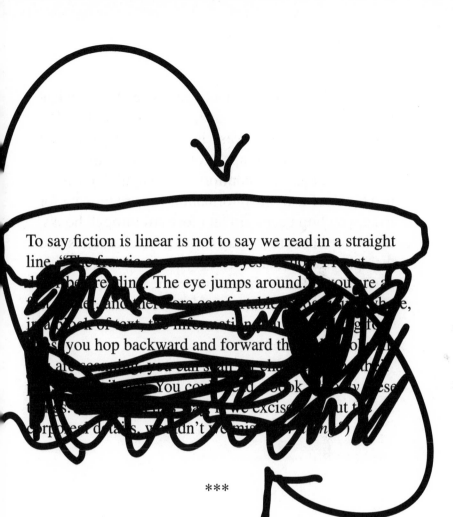

To say fiction is linear is not to say we read in a straight line. "The f... ...the eyes ... ...be reading. The eye jumps around. ...you are a ... and therefore comfortable ... in a book of text, the information ... ...you hop backward and forward th... ...you can s... ...You co... ...book ... ts... ...we excise ...but ... corporeal details, wouldn't we mis... ...)

***

To say fiction is linear is not to say we read in a straight line. Our eyes perform leaps, as do our minds. "The frantic career of the eyes" is how Proust described reading. The eye jumps around. If you are a fast reader, and therefore comfortable recognizing where, in a block of text, the information you are looking for lives, you hop backward and forward through books. If you are scanning, you can scan for characters and their physical attributes. You could read a book for *only* these things. But if we read this way, if we excised all but the corporeal details, wouldn't we miss *everything*?

***

Right: Dr. Zhivago

I

Ren funeral.

The priest,

A ten-year-old boy

. His snub-nosed face   . His neck
stretched out.

A man in black,

SKETCHING

Of course, as Oliver Sacks reminds us in his *Hallucinations*: "One does not see with the eyes; one sees with the mind."

And our minds are unaware of the trip and flutter of our visual organs.

We fix what is a fragmentary draft—we take the sketch that is reading and fill it in, crosshatch, color in the spaces . . .

Our minds synthesize the disparate pieces, and create a painting out of a mere outline. (Though I am using a visual metaphor to describe a process that is semantic.)*

---

*"It is no more essential to the understanding of a proposition that one should imagine anything in connection to it, than that one should make a sketch from it."   —Ludwig Wittgenstein, *The Philosophical Investigations*

The Metamorphosis

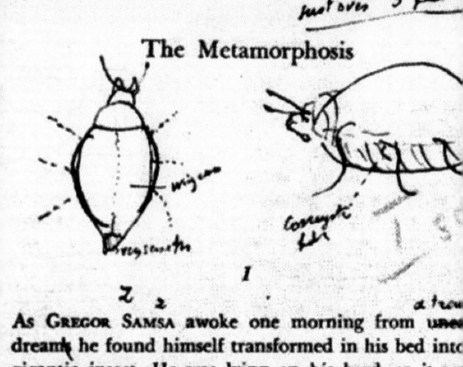

just over 3

wigcan

Gregsamsin

Corrupti tibi

1

Z 2

a trou

As **Gregor Samsa** awoke one morning from ~~unea~~ dream; he found himself transformed in his bed into ~~gigantic~~ insect. He was lying on his hard, as it wo armor-plated, back and when he lifted his head a lit he could see his dome-like brown belly divided into s ~~arched~~ *corrugated* segments on top of which the bed quilt cou hardly keep in position and was about to slide off co pletely. His numerous legs, which were pitifully th compared to the rest of his bulk, ~~waved~~ *flapped* helplessly befo his eyes. *flimmeren*

What has happened to me? he thought. It was dream. His room, a regular human bedroom, ~~or~~ *the* rather ~~too~~ small, lay quiet ~~between~~ *within its* the four famill walls. Above the table on which a collection of clo samples was unpacked and spread out—Samsa was commercial traveler—hung the picture which he h recently cut out of an illustrated magazine and put in a pretty gilt frame. It showed a lady, with a fur cap

Some people *actually* sketch as they read in an attempt to clarify, stabilize, and make fast what they know about the appearances of people or places in a book. Nabokov did this. (On the left is his version of Kafka's Gregor Samsa.)

***

Evelyn Waugh was an illustrator. Poe was a deft portraitist. Hermann Hesse was a skilled painter, as was Strindberg. Emily and Charlotte Brontë drew, as did Goethe, Dostoevsky, George Sand, Victor Hugo, Ruskin, Dos Passos, Blake, Pushkin . . .

Kipling

Poe

Lorca

Baudelaire

Dostoevsky's sketches for *Crime and Punishment*

An author might draw for pleasure. But sometimes for an author, drawing is a heuristic tool. An author will sometimes draw a figure or scene in order to better paint its verbal portrait (sketching might help the author describe a character, as the author can describe his sketch, rather than the nebulous contents of his mind).

Joyce's Leopold Bloom

These drawings are a private matter; they are intended for the author only (as earlier drafts of a novel might be).

Authors can also be idle doodlers. I know Joyce squiggled out a picture of Leopold Bloom but he didn't intend for readers to see this image.*

(This doodle of Joyce's shouldn't inform our reading of his verbal portrait of Leo Bloom, and it certainly bears no resemblance to my own Leo Bloom. Joyce's sketch of Bloom is a caricature.)

And on the whole, the enormous disparity between a great author's verbal talent and his or her artistic efforts

---

*Though he did consent to having Henri Matisse illustrate *Ulysses*. (Matisse clearly never read Joyce's book, and seemed content to render Homer's text instead.)

(Above, a drawing by W. Faulkner. There is nothing to be learned here.)

renders any effort to find cross-medium meaning futile. For instance, Faulkner's prose style and his drawing style are utterly distinct.

Kafka drew what seems to be Josef K, or a similar figure (perhaps Kafka himself?):

The Czech poet Gustav Janouch relates this particular incident, involving Kafka drawing:

As I approached him, he laid the pencil down on the paper which was covered with hastily executed sketches of strange figures.

"You've been drawing?"

Kafka gave an apologetic smile: "No. These are only doodles."

"May I look? As you know, I'm interested in drawing."

"But these aren't drawings to be shown to anyone. They are purely personal, and therefore illegible hieroglyphs."

He took the piece of paper and with both hands pressed it into a ball which he tossed into a wastepaper basket beside the desk.

"My figures have no proper spatial proportions. They have no horizon of their own. The perspective of the shapes I try to capture lies outside of the paper, and the other unsharpened end of the pencil—in myself!"

Much of what Kafka says about his sketches could be applied to his fiction as well. I wonder if Kafka gave a similar rationale when he demanded that Max Brod destroy his writings, the horizons of which also stretch beyond the boundaries of "the paper." This is not to say that Kafka's sketches are as *significant* as his writing, but I wonder if these drawings don't point toward a manner of interpreting Kafka's prose.

***

Some authors make sketches of subject matter from the worlds they've created. Sometimes these sketches are illustrations, meant to accompany texts. (These authors are author-illustrators.) William Thackeray, for instance. Here is one of Thackeray's own illustrations for his *Vanity Fair*:

We readers are relieved of the onus of creating mental pictures for novels and stories that already include actual pictures (illustrated novels). Henry James, in his preface to *The Golden Bowl*, has this to say:

> *Anything that relieves responsible prose of the duty of being, while placed before us, good enough, interesting enough and, if the question be of picture, pictorial enough, above all in itself, does the worst of services . . .*

***

I find that when I'm reading a book with illustrations, the book's pictures will shape my mental visions—but only while I am looking at these illustrations. After a period (which varies in length according to how often the illustrations appear in a text), the particular mental image of that illustration fades.*

*Unless, that is, you are reading a book that has illustrations on every page. In which case there is simply no escaping the imposition of another's imagination. *Ahem.*

Wittgenstein (this time in his *Philosophical Grammar*) writes:

"We do sometimes see memory pictures in our minds: but commonly they are only scattered through the memory like illustrations in a story book."

This sounds right to me, and can apply to imaging while reading as well—though the question remains:

What do we *see* during the *unillustrated* part of the story?

SKILL

A sketch may be judged according to how closely it cleaves to its subject, or it might be judged according to its relative degree of fantasy. But the quality of a sketch will depend most of all upon the skill of the draftsman. Is this true of the images our imaginations construct from narratives as well—our mental sketches? Do some readers have more vivid imaginations than others? Or is the reading imagination a resource with which we are universally, uniformly endowed?

I think of imagination as being like sight—a faculty most people possess. Though, of course, not everyone who is sighted sees with the same visual acuity . . .

1   **A**   20/200

2   **N N**   20/100

3   **A K A**   20/70

4   **R E N I N**   20/50

5   **A A N N A K A**   20/40

6   **R E N I N A A N N**   20/30

7   **A K A R E N I N A A**   20/25

8   N N A K A R E N I N A   20/20

We will sometimes say of someone, "What an amazing imagination they have," by which we mean to say either "How *creative* they are!" or worse, "How *insane* or *duplicitous* they are!" Though in both cases, we are remarking upon a person's ability to conjure something. When we praise an *author's* imagination, I believe that what we are praising is his ability to *transcribe* his visions. (It's not that this author's mind is freer than ours—perhaps it is the opposite: his mind is less wild, and therefore it is easier for him to subdue his thoughts, tame them, and corrall them onto the page.)

189

Do stories and their inhabitants seem sketchy only at those moments in which we are imagining poorly?

Children read picture books; preteens read chapter books with pictures; eventually young adults graduate to books made up entirely of words. This process exists because we learn to read a language slowly, in

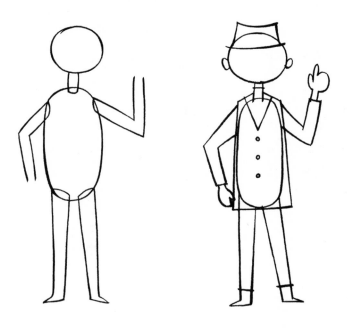

stages, though I wonder if we also need, over time, to learn how to picture narratives unassisted. (The implication being that our imaginations can, and do, improve over time.)

So can we practice imagining—as we practice drawing—in order to *imagine better*?

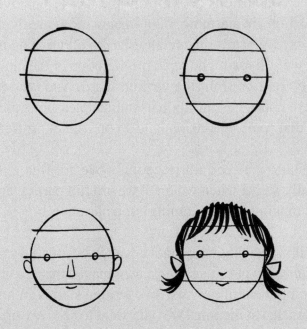

If one reader might imagine better or worse than another reader, then can one culture be better at imagining than another?

Are the muscles we use to imagine growing weaker as our culture ages? Before the age of photography and film did we picture better, more clearly, than we do now? Our mnemonic skills are atrophying and I wonder if our visual creativity might be as well. Our culture's visual overstimulation is widely discussed, and the conclusions drawn from the fact of this overstimulation are alarming. (Our imaginations are dying, some say.) Whatever the relative health of our imaginations, we still read. The rapid proliferation of the image has not kept us from the written word. And we read because books bestow upon us unique pleasures; pleasures that films, television, and so on cannot proffer.

Books allow us certain freedoms—we are free to be mentally active when we read; we are full participants in the making (the imagining) of a narrative.

Or, if it is true that we cannot advance beyond a vague *sketchiness* in our imaginings, then maybe this is a crucial component of why we love written stories. Which is to say that sometimes we only want to see *very little*.

"There were no 'movies' in those days, and the theatre was only occasionally permitted; but on long afternoons, after you had learned to read, you might lose yourself in 'The Scottish Chiefs' to your heart's content. It seems to me that the beauty of this fashion of leisurely reading was that you had time to visualize everything. It was not necessary for you to be told that Helen Mar was beautiful. It was only necessary for her to say, in tones so entrancing that you heard them, 'My Wallace!' to know that she was the loveliest person in all Scotland."   —Maurice Francis Egan, *Confessions of a Book-Lover*

CO-CREATION

Ernst Gombrich tells us that, in viewing art, there is no "innocent eye." There is no such thing in art as the naïve reception of imagery. This is true of reading as well. Like painters, or writers, or even participants in a video game, we make choices—we have *agency*.

When we want to co-create, we read. We want to participate; and we want ownership. We would rather have sketches than verisimilitude—because the sketches, at least, are *ours*.*

***

198

ΌΣ ΤΑ ΚΛΕΙΝ·
ΑΙΝΙΓ ΜΑΤ
ΉΙΔΕΙ ΚΑΙ
ΚΡΑΤΙΣΤΟΣ ΗΝ
ΑΝΗΡ

EX LIBRIS

SIEGMUND FREUD

:d, it is one of the great and wonderful ch
:s of good books," Proust remarks, in his
ding (or, more properly, his book on *Rusk*
g) ". . . that . . . for the author they may be c
usions' but for the reader 'Incitements.'"

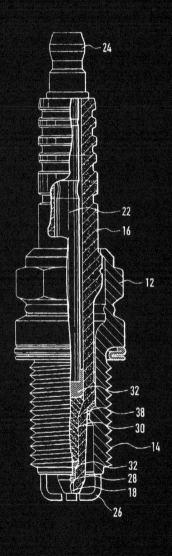

Good books *incite* us to imagine—to fill in an author's suggestions. Without this co-creative act, without personalization, what you are left with is this . . .

←——————————————— Here is your Anna.

(This—the picture to the left—is a form of robbery.)

***

We desire the fluidity and vagary that books grant us when we imagine their content. Some things we do not wish to be shown.

Kafka wrote to the publisher of his *Metamorphosis*, afraid the cover designer might attempt a likeness of his *ungeziefer*:

> *Not that, please not that! The insect itself cannot be depicted. It cannot even be shown from a distance.*

The prohibition is rather frantic. Was Kafka trying to preserve his readers' imaginative acts? One translator of Kafka suggested to me that maybe Kafka wanted his insect seen, by the reader, only *from within—looking out*.

There is another option: visualizing may demand effort on the part of readers, but readers may also *choose* to resist the pictorial in favor of the conceptual.

The more I know of the world (its history, its geography), the closer I get to achieving what we think of as "the author's view of things." I might have visited the Hebrides or read other books that describe the islands. I might have seen illustrations and photographs of period dress, interior décor, and perhaps have learned something of Victorian mores . . . Knowing these things helps me to imagine Mrs. Ramsay's drawing room, dining room, with some degree of verisimilitude.

Perhaps the author's image of this setting is based on some real-world locale that we ourselves can simply see in a photograph or painting? Is this house, the setting for *To the Lighthouse*, based on one of the Woolfs'? I am tempted to look up this information (as another friend of mine did when he read *To the Lighthouse*). It would be a simple matter to find a picture of the Isle of Skye lighthouse. But would this deprive me of something? My vision of the book would gain in authenticity what it would lose in intimacy. (For me, the Ramsays' summer house, filled with guests, is like the rough-and-tumble, rowdy houses my family rents during summers on Cape Cod. This image of the Cape is a grounding image for me. It allows me to relate to the book.) My friend was going to describe the Woolfs' Hebridean house to me and I stopped him. *My* Ramsay house is a feeling, not a picture. And I wish to preserve this feeling. I do not want it supplanted by *facts*.

Well, maybe the house is not *only* a feeling . . . but the feeling has primacy over the image.

The idea of the house, and the emotions it evokes in me, are the nucleus of a complex atom, around which orbit various sounds, fleeting images, and an entire spectrum of personal associations.

These images we "see" when we read are personal: What we *do not see* is what the author pictured when writing a particular book. That is to say: Every narrative is meant to be transposed; imaginatively translated. Associatively translated. It is ours.

***

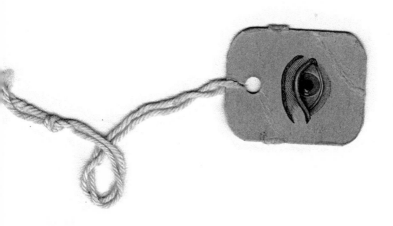

A friend grew up in suburban Albany. He's always been an avid reader, even as a child, and whenever he read, he tells me, he mentally situated the stories in the backyards and side streets of his native blocks, because he had no other frame of reference. I did this too. For me, the settings for most books I read was Cambridge, Massachusetts, where I grew up. So the stage for all of these epic encounters—for *Jean-Christophe*, and, say, *Anna Karenina*, or *Moby-Dick*—was a local public school, my neighbor's backyard . . . It seems strange, funny even, to think of these grand sagas recast in this prosaic light. These various far-flung adventures, press-ganged, by force of will, onto such blasé and unromantic settings. Yet my personal readings of these books were undiminished by radical changes of milieu—by this personalizing of the reading experience. And my friend and I were doing, to some extent, what we all do when we sit down to read a work of fiction.

***

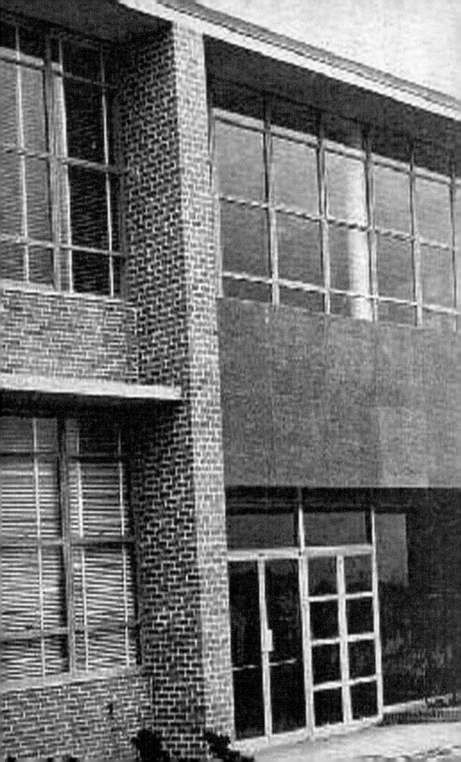

We colonize books with our familiars; and we exile, re-patriate the characters to lands we are more acquainted with.

We transpose works of nonfiction to similar effect.

When I read a book on the battle of Stalingrad, in my imagination the bombardment, occupation, encirclement, and liberation all took place in Manhattan. Or they took place in an alternate Manhattan; a through-the-looking-glass Manhattan; a counterfactual-history Manhattan; a Manhattangrad, consisting of Soviet-mandated architectural adjustments.

The difference here is that, unlike with fictional settings based on real locales, I feel a strange moral obligation to seek out more information about the real Stalingrad. My customized Stalingrad is a false idea. And however my personalizing of the scene helps me identify with the victims of this outsized drama—the actual victims of the actual tragic events—the act of visual substitution seems somehow disrespectful, wrong.*

*Yet I still graft myself into a narrative every time I read nonfiction. How could I not?

When we see plays performed on the stage, we work with a different set of standards. Hamlet is ours to picture as we'd like, as he might be played by a different actor in every new production produced. We do not refer to Hamlet as a character as much as a *role*. He is clearly meant to be inhabited: played. And Denmark is a *set*. It can be anywhere the director and stage designer imagine it to be.

(Perhaps these terms—*role* and *set*—should be used when describing novels?)

Doesn't reading a novel mean producing a private play of sorts? Reading is casting, set decoration, direction, makeup, blocking, stage management . . .

Though books do not imply *enactment* in quite the same way that plays do.

THE READING IMAGINATION

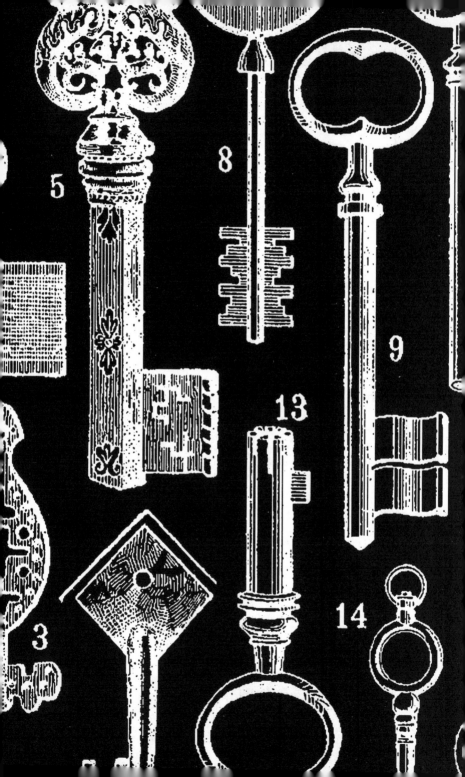

A novelist's objects, places, characters: we want ours to be his, and his to be ours. This desire is paradoxical. It is a desire for *privileged* access, and thus a type of greed. But it is also a hedge against loneliness—the vision is *shared* . . .

(Though perhaps it's better to say that the vision is borrowed? Or even plagiarized?)

Author	DICKENS, CHARLES	
Title	BLEAK HOUSE	
Date Due	Borrower's Name	
	Vladimir Nabokov	

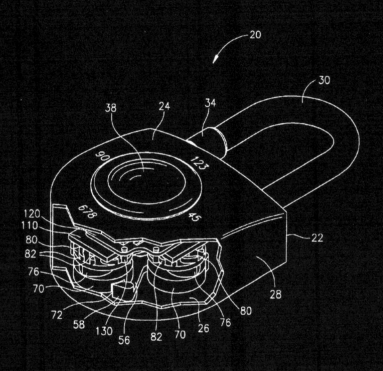

Of course, we also cherish the notion that books hold secrets; that books are *reticent*. (As I've mentioned: books safeguard mysteries.)

Can we picture whatever we'd like when we read? What is the author's role in hemming in the boundaries of our imaginations?

Co-creation and Barthes's "removal of the author":

> *Once the Author is removed, the claim to decipher a text becomes quite futile. To give a text an Author is to impose a limit on that text, to furnish it with a final signified, to close the writing.*

> *The reader is . . . simply that someone who holds together in a single field all the traces by which the written text is constituted.*

The author's "removal" describes not only the passing of one paradigm (of the passive reception of "meaning") but also naturally entails the end of another—the reader's submissive reception of imagery. After all—if we posit the removal of the author—*from whom* would we be receiving imagery?

***

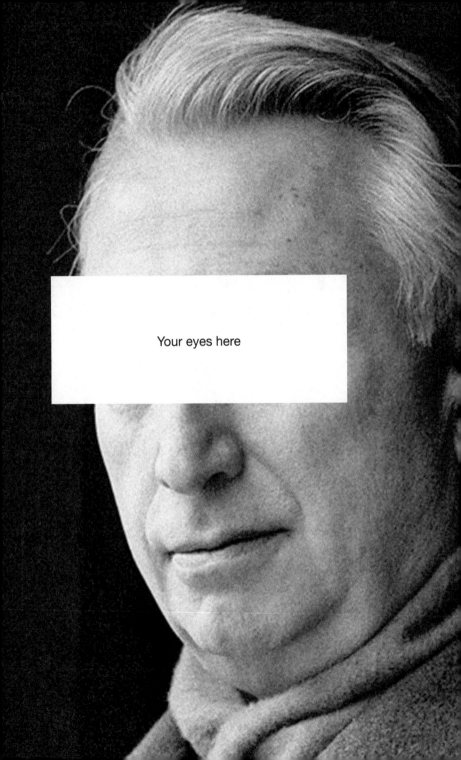
Your eyes here

MAPS
& RULES

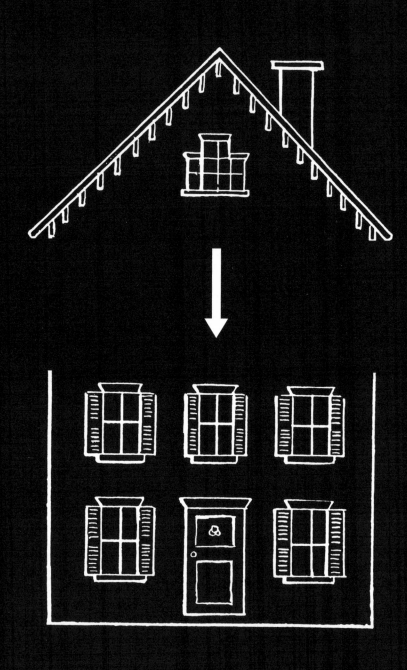

The action in *To the Lighthouse* unfolds at a house in the Hebrides. If you asked me to describe the house, I could tell you some of its features. But much like my mental picture of Anna Karenina, the house is a shutter here, a dormer there.

There's nothing to keep the rain out! Now I picture a roof. I still don't know if it's slate or shingle. Shingle. I've decided. (Sometimes our choices are significant—sometimes not.)

I know that on the Ramsays' property there is a garden, and a hedge. A view of the ocean and the lighthouse. I know the rough placements of the characters on this stage. I have mapped the surroundings, but mapping isn't exactly picturing—not in the sense of re-creating the world, as it appears to us, visually.

(Nabokov also used to *map* novels.)

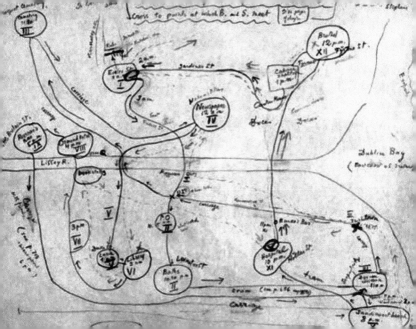

I do this too on occasion. I've mapped *To the Light-house.*

But I still can't describe the Ramsays' house.

Our maps of fictional settings, like our maps of real settings, perform a function. A map that guides us to a wedding reception is not a picture—a picture of what the wedding reception will look like—but rather, it is a set of guidelines. And our mental maps of the Ramsay house are no different—they govern the actions of its occupants.

William Gass (again):

> *We do visualize, I suppose. Where did I leave my gloves? And then I ransack the room in my mind until I find them. But the room I ransack is abstract—a simple schema . . . and I think of the room as a set of likely glove locations . . .*

The Ramsay house is a set of likely *Ramsay* locations.

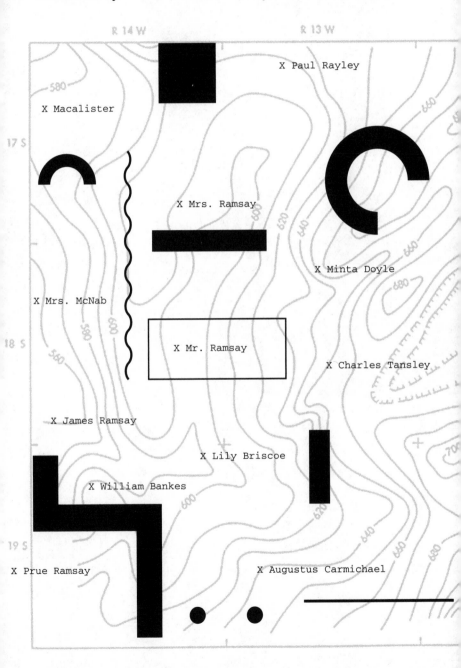

East lie the Iron hills
where is Dain.

the
Lonely
Mountain

Here was Giri
lord in Dal

the

Here of old was Thrain
King under the Mountain

The Desolatior
of Sma

Far
o the North
are
e Grey Mountains
&
Withered Hearth
whence came the

Great Worms.

West lies Mirkwood the Great
there are Spiders

Visibility can be confused with credibility. Some books seem as though they are presenting us with imagery, but are actually presenting us with fictional *facts*. Or rather, these books predicate their plausibility, and for the reader, their conceivability, on an accretion of detail and lore. J. R. R. Tolkien's *Lord of the Rings* trilogy is one such text. The endpapers tell the readers that they might like to know the location of Rivendell, and the appendix suggests that it might be prudent to learn Elvish. (Endpaper maps are always tip-offs that one is entering just such a book/compendium-of-knowledge.)

These books demand scholarship. (The scholarship demanded is a large part of the appeal of such books.) One can learn about the myths and legends of Middle Earth as one can acquaint oneself with its flora and fauna. (One can similarly investigate the fictional worlds of non-fantasy-genre novels—for instance, the "Organization of North American Nations" in David Foster Wallace's *Infinite Jest*.)

Simulacrum worlds such as these require that their constituent parts, their contents, seem *endless*. The authors lead us down a narrative path, but we always have the impression that we could leave that trail and bushwhack, and at the end of our wanderings, we'd find the unlit parts of these worlds intact and replete with nuance.

However: an author does not need to stockpile detail in order to create a credible world (or character).

A shape may be defined by a set of points that lie on its perimeter—nothing more is needed. Or: a rule can be determined.

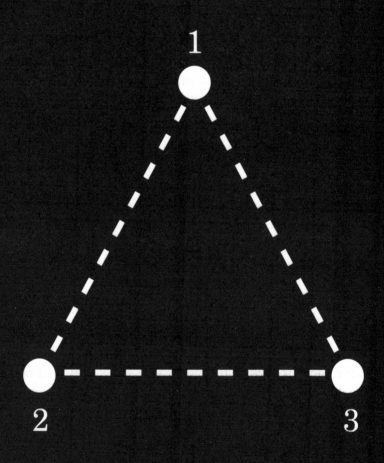

What is crucial in the formulation of a rule or function is its *applicability*. The user must possess the ability to apply the rule forward. (The function, and those who apply it, must be able to "go on.")

The same can be said of, say, a character. Anna can be defined by several discrete points (her hands are small; her hair is dark and curly) or through a function (Anna is graceful*).

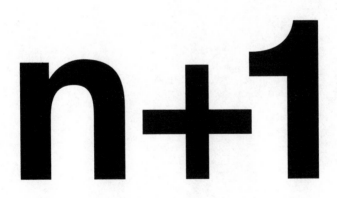

*Unlike how she appears in earlier drafts of the novel, wherein (as Richard Pevear tells us in the introduction to his new translation of the book) Anna is portrayed as "graceless" and rude.

ABSTRACTIONS

Impossible Geometries

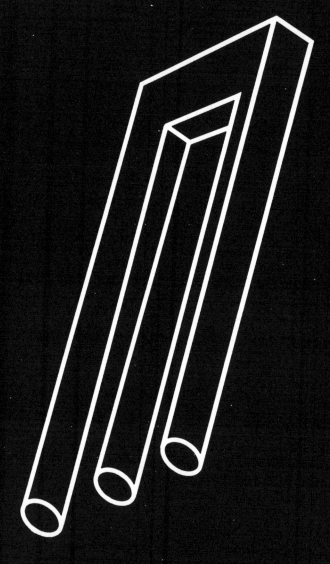

I was reading a book by H. P. Lovecraft when I reached a passage describing "impossible geometries . . ." and "Terrors unutterable and unimaginable."

(Sometimes, when we are reading, we are asked explicitly to imagine the unimaginable.)

> *. . . but in my imagination it was a morbid echo winging its way across unimaginable abysses from unimaginable outer hells.*

Are we being asked *not to see*?

Certain genres are predicated on this convention: science fiction, horror . . .*

In these instances I have a sensation of alienation and eerie astonishment—this is how I perform this act of "not seeing."

Though when I am told I can't imagine, I still imagine. And the content of my imagination in these cases is no more or less clear, or apt, than my visions of Anna Karenina.

***

*or contemporary theoretical physics.

"There is no real unity without incorporeality."

Moses Maimonides writes, in his *Guide for the Perplexed*, that imagining God as "having a body possessed of face and limbs" is impossible. Imagining or describing such a God would entail raising intractable paradoxes and other philosophical and theological difficulties.

Many medieval scholars struggled with this idea—that a "unified" God could not be predicated.

Maimonides subscribed to an approach known as "negative theology" in which one comes closer to God by enumerating the things he is *not*.

Characters have only implied corporeality. And our imaginations grant them unity. But characters are also defined by what they are not.

By asserting that Vronsky

was a squarely built, dark man, not very tall . . .

. . . Tolstoy informs us that Vronsky is neither blond, nor short.

***

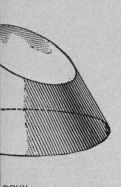

DOLLY

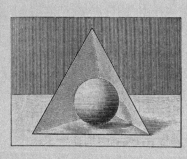

ANNA, VRONSKY

OBLONSKY

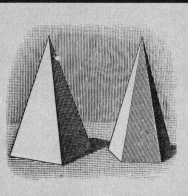

LEVIN, KITTY

PRINCESS BETSY

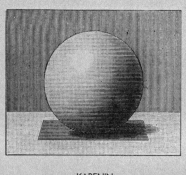

KARENIN

If we don't have pictures in our minds when we read, then it is the interaction of ideas—the intermingling of abstract relationships—that catalyzes feeling in us readers. This sounds like a fairly unenjoyable experience, but, in truth, this is also what happens when we listen to music. This relational, nonrepresentational calculus is where some of the deepest beauty in art is found. Not in mental pictures of things, but in the play of elements . . .

When you listen to music (nonprogrammatic music), is what you feel lessened in any way by the lack of imagery put forward? You may imagine anything when listening to an instrumental fugue by Bach: a stream, a tree, a sewing machine, your spouse . . . but there is nothing in the music that demands those specific images. (I believe that it is far better without them.)

Why is it different when we read a novel? Because some detail, some specific imagery, is called out? This specificity changes things, but, I think, only superficially.

***

Do we visualize anything when we read? Of course, we must visualize something . . . Not all reading is merely abstract, the interplay of theoretical notions. Some of our mental content seems to be pictorial.

Try this thought experiment:

1. Think of the capital letter D.

2. Now imagine it turning ninety degrees counterclockwise.

3. Now take it and mentally place it on top of the capital letter J.

NOW . . . WHAT IS THE WEATHER LIKE, IN YOUR MIND?

(We think "rainy" because we successfully construct and manipulate mental pictures—and here we've demonstrated the fact that we have done so.)

(We made a picture in our minds.)

Of course, the picture we made is a picture of two symbols; letterforms. An actual picture of an umbrella *is much harder to see . . .*

When we are seeing while reading, we are seeing what we are prompted to see.

Though . . .

As John Locke puts it: "Every man has so inviolable a liberty to make words stand for what ideas he pleases, that no one hath the power to make others have the same ideas in their minds that he has . . ."

Yet . . .

This isn't *entirely* true either, is it?

I can, actually, violate this liberty of yours, and force an image, of a kind, to appear to you—just as an author does—as Tolstoy does with Anna and her "masses of hair."

If I say the words:

"Sea horse"

Did you see it? Or imagine that you did? Even for a moment?

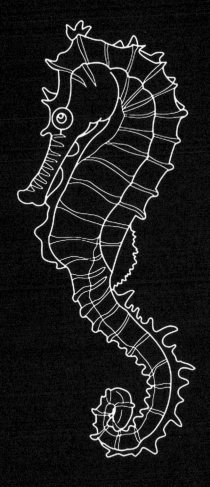

Every imagined sea horse will be different, one from
the next.

But each of these imagined sea horses will share over-lapping series of characteristics; they will share a *family resemblance* (Wittgenstein's phrase) . . .

This is likely true of all our imagined Anna Kareninas, or Madame Bovarys (or Ishmaels) as well. They are not the same, but they are *related*.

(If we averaged all our Annas, would we at last see *Tolstoy's* Anna? I suspect not.)

EYES,
OCULAR VISION,
& MEDIA

John Milton was blind, as was, supposedly, the poet Homer. So too was the fictional prophet Tiresias. Though imagination and insight (*in-sight*) differ from ocular vision, we accept the metaphor of the imagination as a turning inward. Imagination is a turning-away from the mind-independent world.*

We further surmise that outward sight only inhibits inward sight (Homer; Tiresias).

Charlotte Brontë writes, "I feel now as if I had been walking blindfold—this book seems to give me eyes . . ."

*See also *Beethoven*: *deaf*

Imagination, you could say, is like an "inward eye."

Though, as a friend suggests, this implies that the contents of the mind are *there to be seen*—as if ideas were tiny objects. But we don't see "meaning." Not in the same way that we see horses, or apples, or this page that you are looking at now.

William Wordsworth (famously) recounts how he and his sister, Dorothy, saw a stretch of yellow flowers by a lake.

Later (and *often*) these flowers reappear to him:

> *For oft, when on my couch I lie*
> *In vacant or in pensive mood*
> *They flash upon that inward eye*
> *Which is the bliss of solitude . . .*

My father encouraged me to memorize this poem as a child and I've thought about it often since—its representation of percepts; their afterimage; their transmutation into memory, and then art.

Wordsworth's daffodils are remembered, rather than imagined. The flowers, their golden hue and lazy movement, come to the poet at first as sensory information. He receives them (supposedly) *passively*. Only later do these flowers become fodder for reflection and for his active imagination.

By which point Wordsworth has internalized these flowers. But the raw material of the memory is, purportedly, these actual daffodils.

(The very ones Wordsworth saw.)

We have not seen Wordsworth's daffodils "fluttering and dancing in the breeze." We may have seen other daffodils—but we haven't seen his. So we must imagine them, spurred by the poet's words—his mimesis.

But: notice how well the last stanza of this poem describes our acts of imagination as we read Wordsworth's poem—the nebulous yellow of the flowers "flashes" before our own "inward eyes."

***

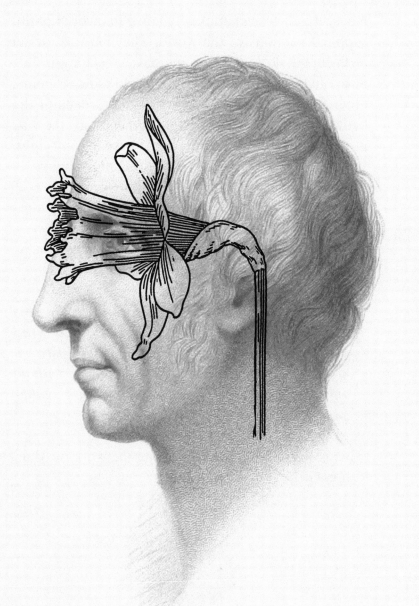

Novels (and stories) implicitly argue in favor of philosophical versions of the world. They assume, or set forth, an ontology, an epistemology, a metaphysics . . . Some fictions assume that the world is as it seems; other fictions tease and worry at the threads of the known. But it is in a novel's phenomenology, the way in which a piece of fiction treats perception (sight, say), that a reader finds a writer's true philosophy.

***

What of a literature that presents us with a nondramatic, optical view of the world, a literature of surfaces?

> . . . *We no longer look at the world with the eyes of a confessor, of a doctor, or of God himself (all significant hypostases of the classical novelist), but with the eyes of a man walking in his city with no other horizon than the scene before him, no other power than that of his own eyes.*

(This is Roland Barthes describing the work of Alain Robbe-Grillet.)

In the works of Robbe-Grillet, objects are shorn of allegorical meaning. They are not symbols, nor are they way stations along an associative chain. They do not mean; nor do they mean nothing.

For Robbe-Grillet, they simply are.

> *A quarter tomato that is quite faultless, cut up by the machine into a perfectly symmetrical fruit. The peripheral flesh, compact, homogeneous, and a splendid chemical red, is of an even thickness between a strip of gleaming skin and the hollow where the yellow, graduated seeds appear in a row, kept in place by a thin layer of greenish jelly along a swelling of the heart. This heart, of a slightly grainy, faint pink, begins—towards the inner hollow—with a cluster of white veins, one of which extends towards the seeds—somewhat uncertainly. Above, a scarcely perceptible accident has occurred: a corner of the skin, stripped back from the flesh for a fraction of an inch, is slightly raised.*

I have had the experience of looking at the world in a nonallusive manner. This state of mind comes on me suddenly, and I'm aware of my topographic position, and am newly alert to geometry. Suddenly the world seems a purely optical phenomenon—it is reduced to light and its vectors—and I have become the camera, rather than the photographer. Chronology is rendered moot, and the constituent fragments of the world are no longer subservient to my psychology, and self-consciousness, but are startlingly present at hand. There is nothing cold or unnatural in this state of being, but rather something strangely preconscious.

Do these states and their fictions compel our imaginative mind to see more, or to see better? (Do we see Robbe-Grillet's tomato with more clarity and richness than we do, say, Eve's apple?)

I don't.

***

When we imagine something from a book, *where* are we situated? Where is (as it were) *the camera*?

Does the angle of observation depend solely upon the voice in which a narrative is cast? For instance, if a story is cast in the *first person*—and especially if a story is set in the present tense—then we readers will naturally see the action "through the eyes" of the narrator. ("My consciousness behaves as though it were the consciousness of another," writes Georges Poulet in his *Phenomenology of Reading*. "I read, I mentally pronounce an I . . . which is not myself.") This is similar with a second-person narration (in which a "you" is directly addressed) and even a first- or second-person *plural* narration (a "we," or a plural "you.")

With a narrative voice in the third person, or even a first-person narrative set in the past tense (as if a friend were recounting a tale), we are naturally "above" or "beside" the action. Our vantage point, like the narrative vantage point, is "godlike."* Perhaps in these cases, we jump from "camera" to "camera," capturing reactions in close-up, and then pull back to see larger "shots," crowd scenes, skylines: the dolly pulls back . . . and even here, despite the omniscient narrative mode, we occasionally slip into the first person (like a god assuming a human avatar) and we see through the eyes of a single character.

*As it is referred to in game design.

But of course, once again, we are speaking of attending the theater, and of watching movies, not reading books. We don't see nearly this much, and an author's choice of narrative *person* changes nothing visually. (The narrative mode changes meaning, but not angle. It doesn't change the way we see . . .)

Ishmael addresses me directly* ("Call me Ishmael"), and though I am sometimes at Ishmael's side, at other points I am high above him, gull-like, watching him stroll the streets of New Bedford. Or I may be seeing, as if through Ishmael's eyes, the shocking first glimpses of his roommate, Queequeg. This is to say: Our vantage point for seeing a narrative is as fluid and unconstrained as the author's imagination in creating it. Our imaginations will roam where they will.

*Or he addresses a generalized "me": i.e., *readers.*

The more we are exposed to film, TV, and video games, the more those types of media infect our readerly perspective. We begin to make films and video games of our readings.

(Video games, I find, are especially potent with regard to this leakage, in that, like reading, they provide the participant with agency . . .)

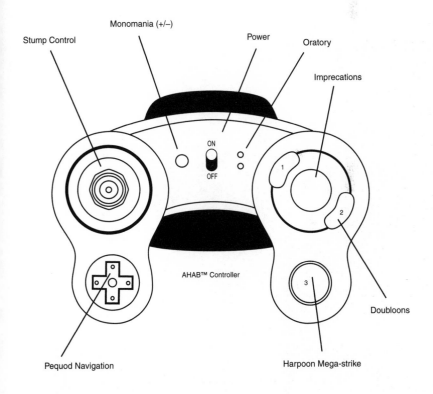

First person.
The hero's vantage.

ONEGIN   LENSKY

1   0

Third person.
The "God's-eye" view.

ONEGIN   LENSKY

1   0

There is no such thing as a "close-up" in prose. A detail may be called out in a narrative, but the effect is not the

same as that of a camera, zooming in. In books, when a detail (Oblonsky's slippers, for instance) is remarked

upon, the observer does not have the sensation of moving closer, or even of a different vantage point.

These events in fiction are not spatial, but semantic. When a camera

zooms in, the relationship of the camera to the object changes and thus

our relationship (as viewers) to the object has changed. *But not in novels.*

As Calvino puts it: "The distance between language

and image is always

the same."*

*Italo Calvino, *Cahiers du Cinema*, October 1966

280

1.48
0.45

8

3.2

This raises an interesting question: Aside from the difficulty of picturing *things*, can we picture a medium or set of dimensions in which things reside, and through which things (and we readers ourselves) imaginatively move? Do we imagine *space*? "Zooming" implies a context for movement—not only does the object of our scrutiny become larger, but a previous scene and its contents must also become diminished . . .

5

1

3

20

7

100
30

8

ft
m

3.5-6.3/18-250

3.5-6.3/18-250

MARCEL PROUST
SWANN IN LOVE

Translated by
C.K. Scott Moncrieff and Terence Kilmartin
Preface by Volker Schlöndorff

$3.95 394-72769-X

When a work of fiction is adapted for the screen, the film will powerfully suppress our own readerly visions of the text . . . but what else can we learn?

Seeing the film of a book is a wonderful test case for exploring our reading imaginations. The contrast in the experiences is revelatory. (Neurologists similarly learn brain function through the study of brain *dysfunction*.)

When I'm reading a novel or story, the contents—places, people, things—of the drama recede and are supplanted by *significance*. The vision of a flowerpot, say, is replaced by my readerly calculation of the meaning and importance of this flowerpot.

We are ever gauging these significances in texts, and much of what we "see" when we read is this "significance." All this changes when a book is adapted . . .

Robbe-Grillet describes the transformation:

. . . The empty chair became only absence or expectation, the hand placed on a shoulder became only the impossibility of leaving . . . But in the cinema, one sees the chair, the movement of the hand, the shape of the bars. What they signify remains obvious, but instead of monopolizing our attention, it becomes something added, even something in excess, because what affects us, what persists in our memory, what appears as essential and irreducible to vague intellectual concepts are the gestures themselves, the objects, the movements, and the outlines, to which the image has suddenly (and unintentionally) restored their reality. *

For a New Novel, translated by Richard Howard

"Flowerpot"

Daffodil
(Narcissus)

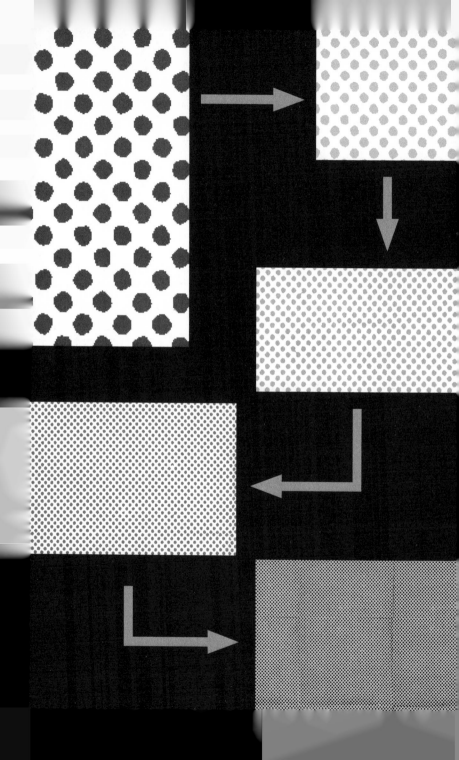

Are novels more like cartoons or comic books than films?

The animated cartoon has a lot to teach the writer, above all how to define characters and objects with a few strokes.*

Not only are characters in novels composed, generally speaking, of "a few strokes," but also, like comic characters, they perform in panels—scenes—which, though not encapsulated by visual frames, are delineated verbally. These scenes/panels are then strung together by the reader, who renders the passages into a plausible narrative whole.

(The void between frames is one of the comic strip's defining characteristics. These fissures serve as a constant reminder of what the comic artist leaves out, while simultaneously drawing attention to the creator's framing power. In fiction, the frames, and thus gaps between frames, are not quite so obvious.)

*Italo Calvino, *The Uses of Literature*

CLASSICS *Illustrated*

DAYS PASS AND INTO THE WINTRY WINDS SAILS THE PEQUOD. BUT STILL NO SIGN OF THE MYSTERIOUS *Captain* AHAB

SUDDENLY ONE DAY...

QUICK, QUEEQUEG. LOOK!

CAPTAIN AHAB!

OLD THUNDER, HIMSELF!

AFTER A FEW MINUTES, STUBB, IN PASSING, DISTURBS THE CAPTAIN ...

WHY DO YOU DISTURB ME, STUBB! DOWN...DOWN TO YOUR KENNEL!

YOU CAN'T CALL ME A DOG, AND GET AWAY WITH IT!

THEN I'LL **CALL** YOU A MULE AND A PIG, TEN TIMES OVER!

NOW GET!

knew he was g
rope's final end
an oarsman, ar
   For an instant
 'The ship? Gre
dim, bewildering
as in the gaseous
of water; while
once lofty perche
sinking look-outs
the lone boat itse
every lance-pole,
and round in one
out of sight.
   But

Authors might draw our attention to the limitations of text—its inability to allow readers simultaneous views of multiple actions, players, and so on.

In the epilogue to *Moby-Dick,* for instance, Ishmael tells us he is:

> . . . *floating on the margin of the ensuing scene, and in full sight of it* . . .

(Notice how "the margin" here becomes like the gap between frames in a comic strip.)

***

MEMORY
& FANTASY

Much of our reading imagination comprises visual free association. Much of our reading imagination is untethered from the author's text.

(We daydream while reading.)

A novel invites our interpretive skills, but it also invites our minds to wander.

ng was vanishing from his sight . . . Inadvertently moving his
: suddenly felt the twenty-kopeck piece clutched in his fist. He
his hand, stared at the coin, swung, and threw it into the water;
turned and went home. It seemed to him that at that moment
ut himself off, as with scissors, from everyone and everything.
:ached home only towards evening, which meant he had been
· for about six hours. Of where and how he came back, he
ered nothing. He undressed and, shivering all over like a spent
y down on the sofa, pulled the greatcoat over him, and imme-
sank into oblivion . . .

e dark of evening he was jolted back to consciousness by
shouting. God, what shouting it was! Never before had he seen
d such unnatural noises, such howling, screaming, snarling,
lows, and curses. He could never even have imagined such
ess, such frenzy. In horror, he raised himself and sat up on his
rmented, and with his heart sinking every moment. But the
, screaming, and swearing grew worse and worse. And then
reat amazement, he suddenly made out his landlady's voice. She
wling, shrieking, and wailing, hurrying, rushing, skipping over
so that it was even impossible to make anything out, pleading
ething—not to be beaten anymore, of course, because she was
nercilessly beaten on the stairs. The voice of her assailant be-
) terrible in its spite and rage that it was no more than a rasp
assailant was also saying something, also rapidly, indistinctly
ig and spluttering. Suddenly Raskolnikov began shaking like a
recognized the voice; it was the voice of Ilya Petrovich. Ilya
ch was here, beating the landlady! He was kicking her, pound-
head against the steps—that was clear, one could tell from the
, the screaming, the thuds! What was happening? Had the
urned upside down, or what? A crowd could be heard gather-
all the floors, all down the stairs; voices, exclamations could be
people coming up, knocking, slamming doors, running. "Bu

The reading imagination is loosely associative—but it is not *random*.

(Our reading imaginations may not be overtly co-
herent, but they are still meaningful.)

So, it occurs to me that perhaps memory—being the fodder of the imagination, and being intermingled with imagination—feels like imagination; and imagination feels like memory, being constructed of *it* as well.

Memory is made of the imaginary; the imaginary made of memory.

I am reading Dickens again (*Our Mutual Friend*), and I'm imagining something from the book—an industrial harbor: a river, boats, wharves, warehouses . . .

From where is the material for my picturing this scene derived? I search my memory to find a similar place, with similar docks. It takes a while.

But then I remember a trip I took with my family when I was a child. There was a river, and a dock—it's the same dock as the dock I just imagined.

I realize later that, when a new friend described to me his home in Spain, with its "docks," I was picturing this same dock—the dock I saw on my childhood vacation; the dock I "used" already in imagining the novel I am reading.

(How many times have I *used* this dock?)

The act of picturing the events and trappings of fiction delivers unintentional glimpses into our pasts.

(And we may search our imaginings, as we search our dreams, for hints and fragments of our lost experience.)

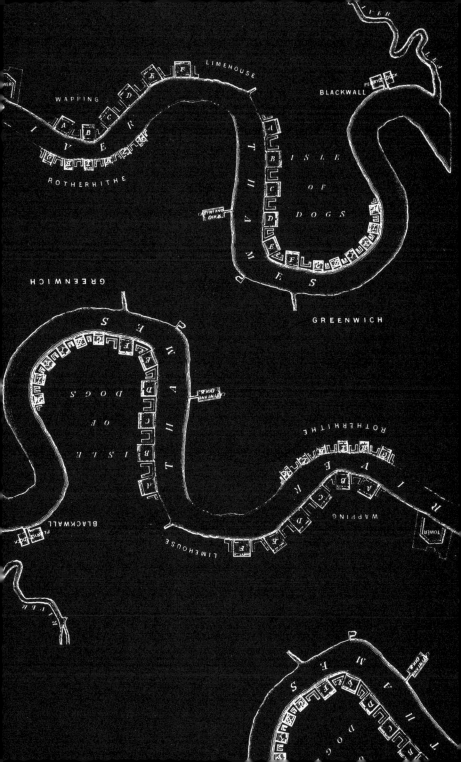

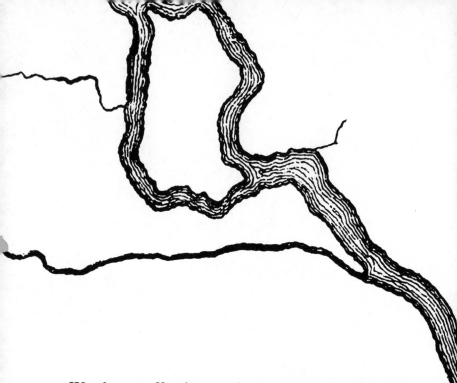

Words are effective not because of what they carry in them, but for their latent potential to unlock the accumulated experience of the reader. Words "contain" meanings, but, more important, words potentiate meaning . . .

***

River, the word, contains within it all rivers, which flow like tributaries into it. And this word contains not only all rivers, but more important all *my* rivers: every accessible experience of every river I've seen, swum in, fished, heard, heard *about*, felt directly or been affected by in any other manner oblique, secondhand or otherwise. These "rivers" are infinitely tessellating rills and affluents that feed fiction's ability to spur the imagination. I read the word *river* and, with or without context, I'll dip beneath its surface. (I'm a child wading in the moil and suck, my feet cut on a river's rock-bottom; or the gray river just out the window, now, just to my right, over the trees of the park—spackled with ice. Or—the almost seismic eroticism of a memory from my teens—of the shift of a skirt on a girl in spring, on a quai by an arabesque of a river, in a foreign city . . .)

This is a word's dormant power, brimming with pertinence. So little is needed from the author, when you think of it.

(We are already flooded by river water, and only need the author to tap this reservoir.)

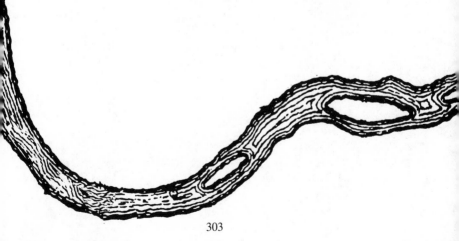

SYNESTHESIA

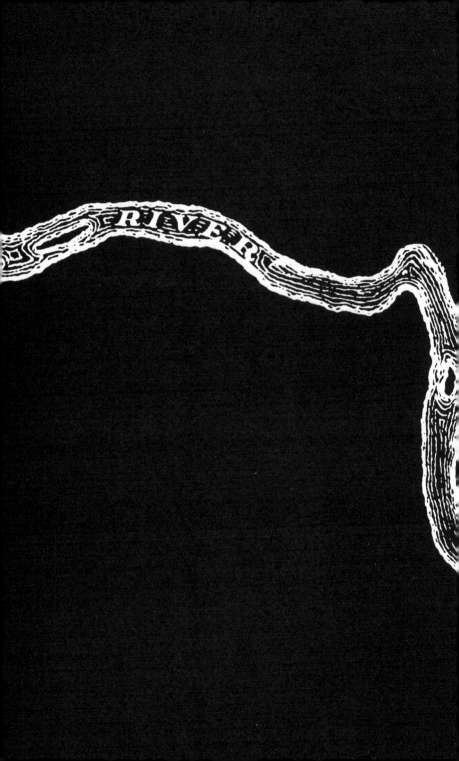

. . . this sleek, sinuous, full-bodied animal, chasing and chuckling, gripping things with a gurgle and leaving them with a laugh, to fling itself on fresh playmates that shook themselves free, and were caught and held again. All was a-shake and a-shiver—glints and gleams and sparkles, rustle and swirl, chatter and bubble.
—Kenneth Grahame, *The Wind in the Willows*

This passage, above, is not so much an evocation of a *vision* of a river* as much as it is an evocation of a feeling: the feeling of *being-happy-beside-a-river.* (A feeling we all might remember.)

Much of what we experience when we read is an over-lapping of, or replacement by, one kind of sensation over another—a synesthetic event. A sound is *seen*; a color is *heard*; a sight is *smelled*; etc. When I mention wading through a river, the "moil and suck" of it, what I mean—and perhaps what you, reading it, might feel—is its eddy, a cool quadrant beneath your knees, and a heaviness of foot . . .

*One of the common metaphors we use when describing the immersive drift of reading is that of floating on a river: we are *carried along* by a narrative, as if we were in an oarless boat. This metaphor implies a passivity that belies the vested involvement of our reading minds. Sometimes we must row hard against the current, or steer around a jutting rock. And even when we are coasting, the boat that is carrying us is: our own minds.

Here is a wonderful character description from Edith Wharton's *House of Mirth*:

> *As she moved beside him, with her long light step, Selden was conscious of taking a luxurious pleasure in her nearness: in the modelling of her little ear, the crisp upward wave of her hair—was it ever so slightly brightened by art?—and the thick planting of her straight black lashes.*

It is helpful that we are told about the shape of this character's hair, and the thickness of her lashes, but what is truly being communicated to us is a rhythm. This rhythm, in turn, conveys a young man's elation at walking alongside a young woman. His growing happiness is communicated not semantically, but sonically—just listen:

"Long light step . . . luxurious pleasure . . . black lashes . . ."

The alliteration of the paragraph practically sings.

"La la la la

(Which is to say that sometimes we confuse seeing and feeling.)

As any poet will tell you, the rhythms, registers, and onomatopoeic sounds of words build a synesthetic transfer in listeners and readers (silent listeners).

From a text arises music.

> *Soft is the strain when zephyr gently blows,*
> *And the smooth stream in smoother numbers flows;*
> *But when loud surges lash the sounding shore,*
> *The hoarse, rough verse should like the torrent roar.*
> *When Ajax strives some rock's vast weight to throw,*
> *The line too labours, and the words move slow;*
> *Not so, when swift Camilla scours the plain,*
> *Flies o'er th' unbending corn, and skims along the main.**

(Another verse I had to memorize in school.)

*Alexander Pope, *An Essay on Criticism*

So we also believe that we hear books; and that we hear them perfectly . . .

Aaron Copland suggested that when we listen to music, we are listening on three "levels": the sensuous, the expressive, and the semantic/musical. The sensuous is, for me, the easiest to forget and the hardest to conjure. If I imaginatively "hear" the opening of Beethoven's Fifth, I recall that insistent, downward-thrusting figuration. I don't hear the "tutti," or the individual instruments that make up the orchestra. I hear the shape of the notes, and their expressive quality. Strangely, I can recall the voices of singers. Is this because we can, ourselves, from our bodies, produce *voice*?

Do we hear characters' voices? (This seems less far-fetched than seeing their faces.) We certainly imagine that we can mentally "hear" our own voices when we aren't speaking.

"Reading in the third millennium BC may . . . have been a matter of hearing the cuneiform, that is, hallucinating the speech from looking at its picture-symbols, rather than visual reading of syllables in our sense."—Julian Jaynes, *The Origin of Consciousness in the Breakdown of the Bicameral Mind*

Earlier we read Proust describing the reading experience as "The frantic career of the eyes . . ."

The quote ends: ". . . and . . . *my voice, which had been
following, noiselessly.*"

We grope our way through the world with the use of cross-sensory analogies—one sense describing another—though most of our analogies are spatial (such that the future is "forward" and quickly vibrating notes are "high"; happy is "up" and sad is "down"). We imagine that stories have "lines," and we coordinate values, valleys, climaxes, as if plotting them on a graph, from one inchoate sense to another.

Kurt Vonnegut proposed such a graph, showing the basic contours of plot, in his lecture "The Simple Shapes of Stories." I've made such graphs myself . . .

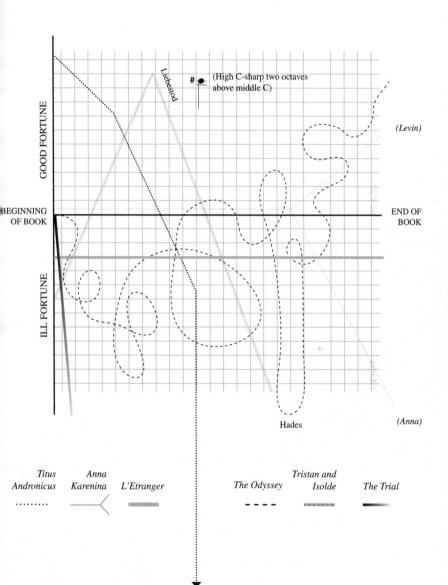

GOOD FORTUNE

Liebestod

\# ● (High C-sharp two octaves above middle C)

(Levin)

BEGINNING OF BOOK

END OF BOOK

ILL FORTUNE

Hades

(Anna)

| *Titus Andronicus* | *Anna Karenina* | *L'Etranger* | *The Odyssey* | *Tristan and Isolde* | *The Trial* |

Laurence Sterne proposed the idea even earlier:

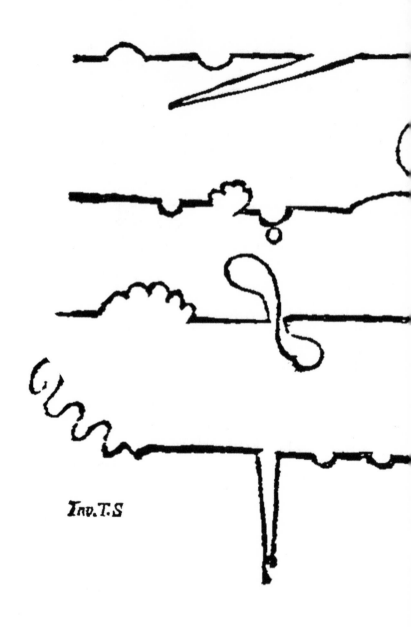

Inv. T. S

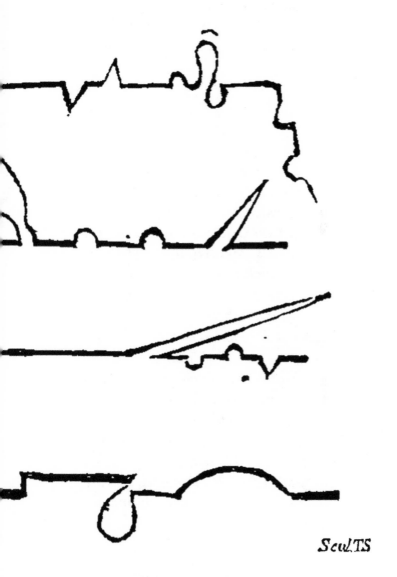

Sculp.TS

Plotlines from, of, *Tristram Shandy*

When I am immersed in a book, my mind begins to formulate corresponding visual patterns . . .

The vectors in Kafka's vision of New York City, from *Amerika*:

From morning to evening and far into the dreaming night that street was the channel for a constant stream of traffic which, seen from above, looked like an inextricable confusion, for ever newly improvised, of foreshortened human figures and the roofs of all kinds of vehicles, sending into the upper air another confusion, more riotous and complicated, of noises, dust and smells, all of it enveloped and penetrated by a flood of light which the multitudinous objects in the street scattered, carried off and again busily brought back, with an effect as palpable to the dazzled eye as if a glass roof stretched over the street were being violently smashed into fragments at every moment . . .

or the mazes of Borges . . .

eral examples I have given; I do know that for many years they plague

ere were corridors that led nowhere, unreachably high windows

grandly dramatic doors that opened onto monklike

palace that I imperfectly explored, the architecture had no purpose

but it was that bright City of the Immortals that terrified and repelled me

Other staircases, clinging airily to the side of a monumental wall, petered

I can no longer know whether any given feature a faithful transcription of reality or one

osely to confuse men; its architecture, prodigal in symmetries, is made

317

or some other or overlapping or undulant thing
for Louis Aragon's *Paysan de Paris* . . .

"I was astonished to see that its window was bathed in a greenish almost subr

that, I remember, emanated from the fish I watched, as a child . . . but still I

properties of creatures of the deep, a physical explanation would still scarc

echoed back from the arched roof. I recognized the sound: it was the same voice of the seashells th

(Though it's hard to say if these shapes are seen, felt, or—merely—understood.)

he source of which remained invisible. It was the same kind of phosphorescence

to myself that even though the canes might conceivably possess the illuminating

or this supernatural gleam and, above all, the noise whose low throbbing

ceased to amaze poets and film-stars. The whole ocean in the Passage de l'Opéra . . ."

SIGNIFIERS

It should be mentioned that there are moments, when we read, when *all we see* are words. What we are looking at when we read *are* words, made up of letterforms, but we are trained to see past them—to look at what the words and letterforms point toward. Words are like arrows—they *are* something, and they also point *toward* something.

Beckett remarked, of James Joyce's *Finnegans Wake*, "it is not written at all. It is not to be read—or rather it is not only to be read. It is to be looked at and listened to. His writing is not about something, it is that something itself."

Words seem transparent to us because of their structure and purpose (they are signifiers) but also because
the practice of reading is *habitual*. We have seen the
"arrow" enough that we look only in the direction in-
dicated.

***

 Tree

 Wood; copse

 Forest

Though there are, in fact, languages that contain pictorial representations of the signified: pictograms; hieroglyphics. In these language systems, the signifier is not arbitrary—the sign shares visual characteristics with its referent. It is a picture of the thing it refers to.

When I see the Chinese character that indicates "tree," for example, I notice the shape of the character, and this shape encourages me to picture a certain kind of tree—of a certain thickness and shape. Similarly, when I see the Chinese character for "forest," the configuration of characters puts me in mind of a certain size of wood—a copse, perhaps. I am responding to the character as a picture.

(But this is only because *I do not speak Chinese.*)

Chinese readers may not "see" the pictures that are constituent parts of their language, because reading Chinese, for them, is habitual (or so I'm told).

A point of interest: The books that make the act of reading feel foreign and nonhabitual are *not* the books in which imaging is most difficult. Or, that is, when we read difficult books, with nontraditional narrative structures, we still imagine that we see.

***

my uncle *Toby*'s story, and my own, in a tolerable straight line. Now,

These were the four lines I moved in through my first, second, third, & fourth volumes.*—In the fifth volume I have been very good,—the precise line I have described in it being this:

By which it appears, that except at the curve, marked A. where I took a trip to *Navarre*,—and the indented curve

B. which is the short airing when I was there with the Lady *Baussiere* and her page,—I have not taken the least frisk of a digression, till *John de la Casse*'s devils led me the round you see marked D.—for as for *c c c c*, they are nothing but parentheses, and the common *ins* and *outs* incident to the lives of the greatest ministers of state; and when compared with what men have done,—or with my own transgressions at the letters A B D—they vanish into nothing.

In this last volume I have done better still—for from the end of *Le Fever*'s episode, to the beginning of my uncle *Toby*'s campaigns,—I have scarce stepped a yard out of my way.

If I mend at this rate, it is not impossible—by the good leave of his grace of *Benevento*'s devils—but I may arrive hereafter at the excellency of going on even thus;

which is a line drawn as straight as I could draw it, by a writing-master's ruler (borrowed for that purpose), turning neither to the right hand or to the left.

This *right line*,—the path-way for Christians to walk in! say divines——

——The emblem of moral rectitude! says *Cicero*——

——The *best line!* say cabbage-planters—is the shortest line, says *Archimedes*, which can be drawn from one given point to another.——

I wish your ladyships would lay this matter to heart, in your next birth-day suits!

——What a journey!

Pray can you tell me,—that is, without anger, before I

Sentences are

also arrows >

. . . and paragraphs and chapters are arrows. Whole novels, plays, and stories are arrows.

incense a flint. Will nothing loose thy tongue? Can nothing melt thee, Or shake thy dogged taciturnity?
TEIRESIAS: Thou blam'st my mood and seest not thine own Wherewith thou art mated; no, thou taxest me.
OEDIPUS: And who could stay his choler when he heard How insolently thou dost flout the State? TEIRESIAS:
Well, it will come what will, though I be mute. OEDIPUS: Since come it must, thy duty is to tell me. TEIRESIAS: I
have no more to say; storm as thou willst, And give the rein to all thy pent-up rage. OEDIPUS: Yea, I am wroth, and will
not stint my words, But speak my whole mind. Thou methinks thou art he, Who planned the crime, aye, and performed it too,
All save the assassination; and if thou Hadst not been blind, I had been sworn to boot That thou alone didst do the bloody deed.
TEIRESIAS: Is it so? Then I charge thee to abide By thine own proclamation; from this day Speak not to these or me. Thou art
the man, Thou the accursed polluter of this land. OEDIPUS: Vile slanderer, thou blurtest forth these taunts, And think'st for-
sooth as seer to go scot free. TEIRESIAS: Yea. I am free, strong in the strength of truth. OEDIPUS: Who was thy teacher?
not methinks thy art. TEIRESIAS: Thou, goading me against my will to speak. OEDIPUS: What speech? repeat it and
resolve my doubt. TEIRESIAS: Didst miss my sense wouldst thou goad me on? OEDIPUS: I but half caught thy
meaning; say it again. TEIRESIAS: I say thou art the murderer of the man Whose murderer thou pursuest. OE-
DIPUS: Thou shalt rue it Twice to repeat so gross a calumny. TEIRESIAS: Must I say more to aggravate thy

M o n -
ster! Thy
silence would

rage? OEDI-
PUS: Say
all thou
wilt:
i t

Oedipus, the play, to me, points
downward.

To read is: to look *through*; to look *past* . . . though also, to look, myopically, hopefully, *toward* . . .

There is very little looking at.

***

BELIEF

When reading *To the Lighthouse*, we come across this sentence:

"While it drew from the long frilled strips of seaweed pinned to the wall a smell of salt and weeds . . ."

Can you smell this odor? When I read this passage I imagined I did. Of course, what I was "smelling" was the *idea* of a smell. Not something visceral like a real smell. *Can* we imagine smells? I posed this question to a neuroscientist, an expert in how the brain constructs "smell."

He said:

I have not met the person who can convincingly tell you that they can re-create peppermint or lilac at will and with . . . immediacy. I myself cannot, but can force a small fragment of the experience in an almost intellectual way—not the visceral experience . . . Why is this? I think that smell . . . has a more primitive, somatic nature: you cannot create the qualities of intense pain or itch in your mind and feel them with any intensity either. Perhaps this is because smell is a primitive stimulus . . . in some ways, the more primitive sensations are more important to survival. The body does not want you to create the experience of smelling danger or food or a mate ex nihilo unless they are actually present—it costs to act, and false alarms can lead to problems.

When we imagine, our experiences of sensations are dulled, so as to distinguish these imagined senses from real cues. We "force" an experience in "an almost intellectual way."

What interests me here is that most people believe they can imagine smells perfectly; viscerally. Or, while they are reading, they tell themselves that *they have smelled something.*

(We have read a book—that is to say: *imagined* it—perfectly.)

The smell of "salt and weeds":

I am not smelling them *as such*. I am performing a syn-esthetic transformation. From the words "smell of salt and weeds" I am calling up an idea of a summer house by the sea, where I've stayed. The experience does not contain any true recall of an odor. It is a *flash*, which leaves a slight afterimage. It is spectral and mutating. An aurora.

A nebula of illusory material.

***

A sticking point—if I tell someone that I do not believe they can (viscerally) conjure a smell from memory, they are affronted. It is terrifying and disorienting that we can't recapitulate the world in perfect facsimile. The metaphors we use to describe our minds, our memories, our very consciousness, are hard to relinquish. Reading a novel, we tell ourselves, is like watching a movie. Remembering a song is like sitting in an audience. If I say the word *onion* you are transported—as if smelling an onion all over again. It bothers people to suggest that this isn't the case.

***

Someone might say, "Well, perhaps *you* can't summon a smell (or sound) by memory, but maybe your sense of smell (or hearing) is poor." (Fair enough.) "But maybe someone with a highly developed sense of smell can summon a scent viscerally—a sommelier, say, or a perfumer . . ."

A sommelier will have more responsive, complex olfactory responses than I do. As a result, a sommelier will have a better, more complete intellectual armature for his recall of scent—he will have a rich taxonomy of smells upon which to draw, and many metrics with which to judge and categorize. One scent may be acrid and lightly fruity. Another spicy and sour, lying upon a spectrum familiar only to experts. This knowledge, though, is no more than a mental trellis upon which to hang the vines of one's olfactory memories.

But these vines don't flower or bear fruit. Not in our minds.

***

I am a visual person (so I am told). I am a book designer, and my livelihood depends not only on my visual acuity in general, but on my ability to recognize the visual cues and prompts in texts. But when it comes to imagining characters, daffodils, lighthouses, or fog: I am as blind as the next person.

***

Perhaps our ability to picture, smell, hear clearly while we read depends on the strength of our faith in our ability to do so? Thinking we can picture, for all intents and purposes, is the same as picturing.

We subscribe to the belief (we have faith) that when we read we are, passively, receiving *visions* . . .

And I looked, and, behold, a whirlwind came out of the north, a great cloud, and a fire infolding itself, and a brightness was about it, and out of the midst thereof as the color of amber.

Maybe the reading imagination is a fundamentally mystical experience—irreducible by logic. These visions are like revelations. They hail from transcendental sources, and are not *of* us—they are visited *upon* us. Perhaps the visions are due to a metaphysical union of reader and author. Perhaps the author taps the universal, and becomes a medium for it. (Perhaps the process is *supernatural*?)

And when I turned I saw seven golden lampstands, and among the lampstands was someone like a son of man, dressed in a robe . . . The hair on his head was white like wool, as white as snow, and his eyes were like blazing fire.

Perhaps the very notion that readers are "see-ers" and the conventions we use to describe the reading experience derive from this tradition—the tradition of visitation, annunciation, dream vision, prophecy, and other manifestations of religious or mystical epiphany . . .

Angels, demons, burning bushes, muses, dreams, seizures, drug-induced reveries . . .

Dream vision (Geoffrey Chaucer):

> *And in my slepe I mette, as I lay,*
> *How African, right in that selfe aray*
> *That Scipioun him saw before that tyde,*
> *Was comen, and stood right at my beddes syde*

Poetic vision (Blake):

> *And by came an angel, who had a bright key, And*
> *he opened the coffins, and set them all free*

Narcotic vision (Thomas De Quincey):

> *"A theatre seemed suddenly opened and lighted up*
> *within my brain, which presented nightly spectacles*
> *of more than earthly splendour."*

Hallucination (Shakespeare):

> *Is this a dagger which I see before me,*
> *The handle toward my hand?*

Epileptic vision (Dostoyevsky):

> *His brain seemed to catch fire at brief moments . . .*
> *His sensation of being alive and his awareness in-*
> *creased tenfold at those moments which flashed by*
> *like lightning. His mind and heart were flooded by*
> *a dazzling light.*

Dream

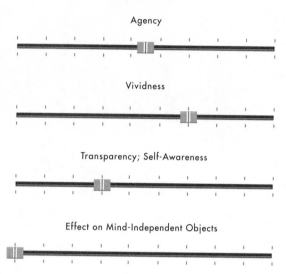

Hallucination

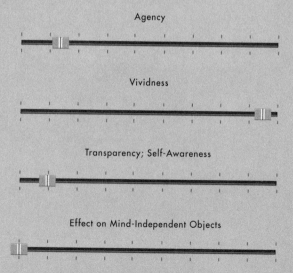

Veridical Perception

Agency

Vividness

Transparency; Self-Awareness

Effect on Mind-Independent Objects

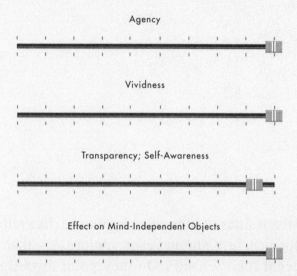

Reading Imagination

Agency

Vividness

Transparency; Self-Awareness

Effect on Mind-Independent Objects

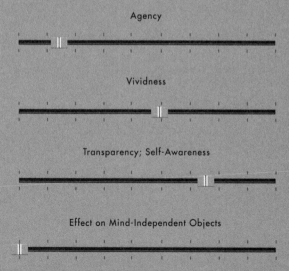

Can the visions of literature claim to be, like religious epiphanies, or platonic verities, more *real* than phenomenal reality itself? Do they point toward some deeper manner of authenticity? (Or: by mimicking the real world, do they point toward *its* inauthenticity?)

MODELS

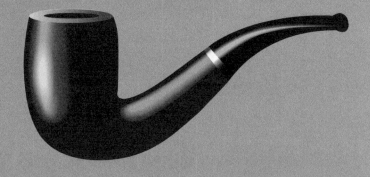

Ceci n'est pas la pipe du Stubb

When we read about something—a place, a person— we separate it from the mass of entities that surround it. We distinguish it. We excise it from the undifferenti- ated. Think of Stubb's pipe. Or Achilles's shield. (This thing is different from all other things: this thing is not Ahab's peg leg, or Hector's helmet.) We then form some kind of mental representation of it. It is a pipe: like this, and not like that. We form representations, so we can remember, and manipulate the memory of this pipe, so the information can be reused. This represen- tation is a model of some sort. So we readers are also model builders.

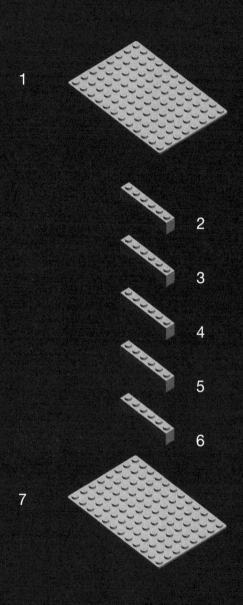

1

2

3

4

5

6

7

Jean Piaget tells us that thought is "mental representation."

But what *kind* of representation? Codes? Symbols?
Words? Propositions? Pictures?

***

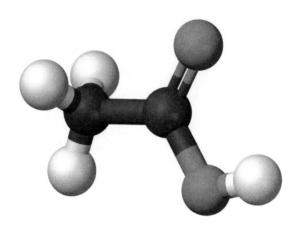

$$x^2 + px + q = 0$$
$$x_{1/2} = -\frac{p}{2} \pm \sqrt{\left(\frac{p}{2}\right)^2 - q}$$
$$f_r = \frac{1}{2\pi} \cdot \frac{1}{\sqrt{LC}}; \quad \omega = 2\pi f_r$$
$$-\frac{d}{dt}\int_A B\,dA = \oint_L E'\,dl = -\int_A \left(\frac{\partial B}{\partial t} + rot(B \times v)\right) dA$$
$$HCl + H_2O \rightleftharpoons Cl^- + H_3O^+$$
$$V = \frac{1}{6}\pi h\left(3e_1^2 + 3e_2^2 + h^2\right)$$

$$W = \int_{s_1}^{s_2} F(s) \cdot \cos\alpha\, ds$$
$$\tanh x = \frac{e^x - e^{-x}}{e^x + e^{+x}}$$
$$u_C = U\left(1 - e^{-t/RC}\right)$$
$$4\,FeS_2 + 11\,O_2 \rightarrow 2\,Fe_2O_3 + 8\,SO_4$$

$$v = \frac{ds}{dt}$$
$$\theta = I \cdot N$$
$$C + O_2 \rightarrow CO_2$$
$$x \parallel y; \quad z \perp x$$
$$W_{rot} = \frac{1}{2} \cdot J\omega^2$$
$$a^2 = b^2 + c^2$$
$$P_v = \int_{r=0}^{2\pi}\int_{\vartheta=0}^{\pi} \frac{r^2}{16\varepsilon_2} H_\varphi H_\varphi^* \sin\vartheta\, d\vartheta\, d\varphi$$

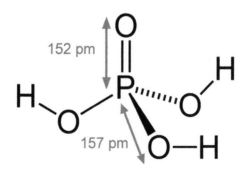

EQUOS

ARBOR

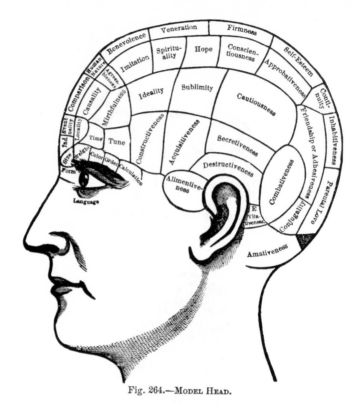

Fig. 264.—MODEL HEAD.

NAMES, NUMBERS AND LOCATION OF THE MENTAL ORGANS.

1. **AMATIVENESS.**—Connubial love, affection.
A. **CONJUGAL LOVE.**—Union for life, pairing instinct.
2. **PARENTAL LOVE.**—Care of offspring, and all young.
3. **FRIENDSHIP.**—Sociability, union of friends.
4. **INHABITIVENESS.**—Love of home and country
5. **CONTINUITY.**—Application, consecutiveness.
E. **VITATIVENESS.**—Clinging to life, tenacity, endurance.
6. **COMBATIVENESS.**—Defence, courage, criticism.
7. **DESTRUCTIVENESS.** — Executiveness, push, propelling power.
8. **ALIMENTIVENESS.**—Appetite for food, etc.
9. **ACQUISITIVENESS.**—Frugality, economy, to get.
10. **SECRETIVENESS.**—Self-control, policy, reticence.
11. **CAUTIOUSNESS.** — Guardedness, care-taking, safety.
12. **APPROBATIVENESS.**—Love of applause and display.
13. **SELF-ESTEEM.**—Self-respect, dignity, authority.
14. **FIRMNESS.**—Stability, perseverance, steadfastness.
15. **CONSCIENTIOUSNESS.**—Sense of right, justice.
16. **HOPE.**—Expectation, anticipation, perfect trust.
17. **SPIRITUALITY.**—Intuition, prescience, faith.
18. **VENERATION.**—Worship, adoration, deference.
19. **BENEVOLENCE.**—Sympathy, kindness, mercy.

20. **CONSTRUCTIVENESS.**—Ingenuity, invention, tools.
21. **IDEALITY.**—*Taste*, love of beauty, poetry and art.
B. **SUBLIMITY.**—Love of the grand, vast, magnificent.
22. **IMITATION.**—Copying, aptitude for mimicry.
23. **MIRTH.**—Fun, wit, ridicule, facetiousness.
24. **INDIVIDUALITY.**—Observation, curiosity to see.
25. **FORM.**—Memory of *shape*, looks, persons, things.
26. **SIZE.**—Measurement of quantity by the eye.
27. **WEIGHT.**—Control of motion, balancing.
28. **COLOR.**—Discernment, and love of colors, hues, tints.
29. **ORDER.**—*Method*, system, going by *rule*, arrangement.
30. **CALCULATION.**—Mental arithmetic, numbers.
31. **LOCALITY.**—Memory of place, position, travels.
32. **EVENTUALITY.**—Memory of facts, events, history.
33. **TIME.**—Telling *when*, time cf day, dates, punctuality
34. **TUNE.**—Love of music, sense of harmony, singing.
35. **LANGUAGE.**—*Expression* by words, signs or acts.
36. **CAUSALITY.**—*Planning*, thinking, philosophy
37. **COMPARISON.**—Analysis, inferring, illustration.
C. **HUMAN NATURE.**—Sagacity, perception of motives.
D. **SUAVITY.**—*Pleasantness*, blandness, politeness.

What are we modeling when we make mental representations of literary characters? *Souls?*

I continue to interrogate readers . . . I ask them to describe a central fictional character (making sure to only discuss books they've just recently finished reading, or have reread several times, so that whatever imagery they conjured when reading would still be fresh in their minds). My subjects respond by offering up one or two physical characteristics of a character (for instance, "He's short and bald—I know *that* much"), followed by a longer disquisition on the character's persona ("He's a coward, unfulfilled, regretful," et cetera). I generally have to stop them at some point in order to remind them that I was asking only for physical description.

That is to say, we confuse what a character *looks like* with who a character, putatively, *is*.

In this way we are backward phrenologists, we readers. We extrapolate physiques from minds.

***

"A great nose may be an index of a great soul."
—Edmond Rostand, *Cyrano de Bergerac*

Buck Mulligan (remember him? He is the character who appears at the opening of Joyce's *Ulysses*) . . .

Other things we know about him . . .

He is, variously:

> "Equine" faced; "sullen" of jowl; "strong" and "well-knit"; light haired; white-toothed; "smokeblue" eyed; "Impatient"; older than his occasional flush makes him appear; gowned; waist-coated; panama-hatted; frowning; "wheedling"; "coarsely vigorous"; "broadly smiling"; "erect"; "ribald"; "solemn as a dean"; "heavy"; "gleeful"; "pious"; "grave"; full of "honeyed malice . . ."

None of these descriptors helps me to picture Buck (some of them seem downright contradictory: his being "plump" and his "equine" face, for instance).

And these depictions of Buck *could* portray practically anyone. But it is Buck's introductory epithet—*stately, plump*—that defines him. But not as a picture. That description becomes, for me, a designation of *type*.

(This "stately" and this "plump" are like categories, in that they don't describe so much as they characterize.)

The novel is, among other things, a *typology* . . .

I notice that we don't praise the *descriptive richness* of fables (in direct contrast to what many readers find commendable in novels and stories). Here, characters are the transparently generalized types.

The flatness of characters and settings in fables and parables—their purposefully two-dimensional, cartoonish aspect—allows such literary systems to function properly. What is important in these cases is universal applicability—as opposed to, say, psychological detail. This is true to the extent that we readers, when we read such tales, might become: a fox; a hawk; a grasshopper; a satyr; a stag.

(In fables, the stylized visual aspect of the players and settings is obvious to us. Yet even the most psychologically rich characters and lushly described locales in naturalistic fiction are, visually: flat.)

Knight-Errant, Harlequin, Mad Scientist, Evil Clown, Elderly Martial-Arts Master, Gumshoe, Action Hero, Crone, Whi Hunter, Spinster, Space Nazi, Reluctant Hero, Ingenue, Nerd, Diva, Redshirt, Hooker-with-a Heart-of-Gold, Battle-Ax Absent-Minded Professo Town Drunk, Southern Belle, Lone Drifter, Roué Blind Prophet, Jezebel, Village Idiot, Everyman Martian

Are *all* characters, in *all* types of fiction, merely visual types, examplars of particular categories—sizes; body shapes; hair colors . . . ?

This doesn't feel true to me as I'm reading a novel. Good characters feel unique. But this uniqueness is only a psychological uniqueness. As I've mentioned many times, authors relinquish little information concerning a character's appearance—thus it's hard to imagine these characters as visually unique, one from the next. It's hard to imagine them aquiring visual *depth*.

Yet somehow they seem to.

"The 'Redskinnery' was what really mattered . . . take away the feathers, the high cheek-bones, the whiskered trousers, substitute a pistol for a tomahawk, and what would be left? For I wanted not the momentary suspense but that whole world to which it belonged—the snow and the snow-shoes, beavers and canoes, warpaths and wigwams, and Hiawatha names."
—C. S. Lewis, *On Stories*

And how does a character or setting acquire this seeming *depth*? How does a verbal construction become *felt*?

How do they emerge as complete in our minds? How do they become, visually

Whole?

THE PART
& THE WHOLE

I'm reading *The Iliad*, and I notice (at this point: unsurprisingly) that Homer gives his character Achilles very few physical attributes. Much of what I know of Achilles in my reading is extrapolated.

Luckily (lest I mistake Achilles for someone else; say, *Patroclus* . . .), Achilles comes with an epithet attached to him. Achilles is "swift-footed."

This epithet is like a name tag. (A Homeric epithet is also a mnemonic device for the reader and the poet alike.) The goddess Athena is given an epithet as well: she is "gray-eyed," *glaucopis*. (She is also "white-armed.") The goddess Hera is "Ox-eyed."

(I've always loved the balefulness of this image—it adds a sympathetic psychological depth to a goddess traditionally characterized as a shrill and jealous harridan.)

These various epithets are more formalized than descriptions.

Homeric epithets are more often than not pictorial—moreover, they are also often *picturesque*. Being picturesque makes them memorable.*

***

---

*What, for example, does a "wine-dark" sea look like? This has been a subject of much debate. Is a wine-dark sea a green or blue sea touched with the roseate colors of the sunset or sunrise? Is Homer's ocean blue? Or did it appear red to him? Did the Greeks have the capacity to *see* blue? Goethe in his *Theory of Color* mentions that colors were less strictly defined for the ancient Greeks: "Pure red (purpur) fluctuates between warm red and blue, sometimes inclining to scarlet, sometimes to violet." So was the sea "wine-dark" for Homer because it "looked that way"? Or because "wine-dark" was rythmically helpful to the poet—or because it was a memorable epithet?

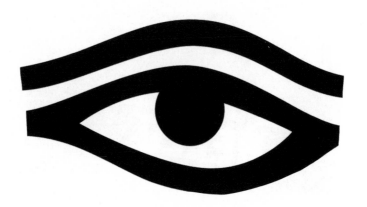

"Gray-eyed" and "Ox-eyed" are not mere imagistic details. When one hears "Ox-eyed Hera" one does not picture a floating set of heavy-lidded eyes.

Hera's eyes, to some extent, stand in for the entire character: they are *parts* of her that are proxies for the totality of her. Hera's eyes are an instance of what is called metonymy. Metonymy is a figure of speech in which one thing (or idea) is called by the name of another thing (or idea) to which it is related. Generally speaking, this related idea is *salient*. For instance, the Pentagon . . .

. . . refers to a building, but more important, it refers to the United States' military leadership that is housed in that building. The building is like a synonym; a related, associated concept that becomes *a stand-in* for the Department of Defense. Similarly, the expression "the White House" refers to the entire presidential staff, and (pulling the lens back farther) "Washington" stands in for the entire U.S. government. Here, concrete facts (geographical locations, buildings) are proxies for more elaborate and convoluted notions.

***

Hera's eyes are an instance of metonymy . . .

But more specifically, Hera's eyes are an instance of *synecdoche*—a synecdoche is a metonym in which the *part* refers to the *whole*.

For instance: Men (sailors) can become "Hands . . ."

"All hands on deck!"

Or: "Nice *wheels* . . ."

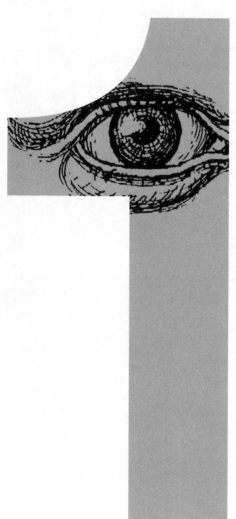

Hera's eyes are atomic components, which represent and fill in for a greater molecular complexity. (We do not consider characters as assemblages of parts, any more than we conceive of real people as aggregates of separate components. We conceive of people/characters as wholes—monads.)

I conceive of myself as "one," not "many."

For Anna Karenina, her "shining gray eyes" *are* Anna;
the piece of her we readers grasp. Her eyes are like
Hera's: they are synecdochic; they are her epithets.

Metonymy, like metaphor, is thought by some to be a part of our innate language faculty—and an even greater foundational aspect of a human being's natural cognitive abilities. (Our understanding of the *part-for-whole* relationship is an important tool by which we understand our world and communicate that understanding to others.) As embodied creatures, we consist of corporeal forms, physiques, which are in turn composed of parts. Being born with a body entails being born with some natural abstract sense of this relationship—of synecdoche.

(Look at your fingernail: You are, in some senses, this fingernail, but your fingernail is also part of you.)

This inborn ability to extrapolate a whole from a part is fundamental and reflexive, and understanding the part-whole structure enables us, somehow, to *see* characters, to see narrative, just as it enables us to function, mentally, physically, in the world.

***

Taking a part for a whole is a kind of substitution.

Metaphors and analogies, like metonymies, are also substitutions.

When Romeo compares Juliet to the sun in Shakespeare's play, he is making an analogy (Juliet is *like* the sun) but he is also letting the sun replace Juliet (Juliet *is* the sun), such that he may use the metaphor to generate further information and understand other relationships, both abstract and concrete. (Rosaline is like the moon, for instance.) The metaphoric Juliet thus supersedes the character "Juliet," a personified Juliet being too complex to mentally encompass. Juliet being the sun thereby becomes another name tag.

SOME OF THE METAPHORS USED IN THIS BOOK TO DESCRIBE THE READING EXPERIENCE:

Arch
Arrow
Atom
Audience
Aurora
Bathtub
Bridge
Camera
Candle
Cartoon
Car trip
Chair
Clock
Cloister
Coin
Computer program
Conductor
Contest
Dam
Dream
Eye
Eye (inward)
Eyelid
Family tree
Film
Fog
Function
Funnel
Game of chess
Glass of water
Glasses
Hallucination

Knife
Library book
Line
Locked room
Magnifying glass
Map
Maze
Metaphor itself
Microscope
Model-building
Molecule
Music
Orchestra
Psychotherapy
Puzzle
Religious vision
River
Road
Road sign
Role-playing game
Rorschach blot
Rulebook
Sketch
Spotlight
Textbook
Vector
Video game
Walk
Wall
Wine

Epithets and metaphors are not names, but neither are they descriptions. Which aspect of a character an author chooses to represent them with is crucial. This is a method by which the author further *defines* his characters. If Buck Mulligan is "stately, plump," it is for an important reason.

As I mentioned, this technique, the use of epithets, may be the method through which we define the (actual) people around us . . . we push an attribute of theirs to the fore; we "foreground" a piece of them and then let that piece suffice. (I have a friend, and when I think of him, I see only his glasses.)

And I wonder . . .

How could we do otherwise?

Without such tools, the world would be presenting us, constantly, with occasions so abundantly and elaborately informative as to be crippling.

ndantly elaborately

and informative

elaborately abundantly

to be abundantly

informative as crippling

native abundantly

abun to be undan

crippling

and as

elaborate

informative

to be crippling.

crippling. to be

to be crippling. to be

cripplingcrippling

IT IS

BLURRED

The world, as we read it, is made of fragments. Discontinuous points—discrete and dispersed.

(So are we. So too our coworkers; our spouses; parents; children; friends . . .)

We know ourselves and those around us by our readings of them, by the epithets we have given them, by their metaphors, synecdoches, metonymies. Even those we love most in the world. We read them in their fragments and substitutions.

The world for us is a work in progress. And what we understand of it we understand by cobbling these pieces together—synthesizing them over time.

It is the synthesis that we know. (It is all we know.)

And all the while we are committed to believing in the totality—the fiction of seeing.*

* *Vision itself*, binocular vision, is a fiction—a synthesis—in which we combine two distinct optical views of the world (while subtracting our noses).

Phantasms;
simulacra;
trails;
splinters;
wreckages . . .

When we apprehend the world (the parts of it that are legible to us), we do so one piece at a time. These single pieces of the world are our conscious perceptions. What these conscious perceptions consist of, we don't know, though we assume that our experience of the world is an admixture of that which is already present, and that which we ourselves contribute (our selves—our memories, opinions, proclivities, and so on).

Authors are curators of experience. They filter the world's noise, and out of that noise they make the purest signal they can—out of disorder they create narrative. They administer this narrative in the form of a book, and preside, in some ineffable way, over the reading experience. Yet no matter how pure the data set that authors provide to readers—no matter how diligently prefiltered and tightly reconstructed—readers' brains will continue in their prescribed assignment: to analyze, screen, and sort. Our brains will treat a book as if it were any other of the world's many unfiltered, encrypted signals. That is, the author's book, for readers, reverts to a species of noise. We take in as much of the author's world as we can, and mix this material with our own in the alembic of our reading minds, combining them to alchemize something unique. I would propose that this is why reading "works": reading mirrors the procedure by which we acquaint ourselves with the world. It is not that our narratives necessarily tell us something true about the world (though they might), but rather that the practice of reading feels like, and *is* like, consciousness itself: imperfect; partial; hazy; co-creative.

***

Among the great mysteries of life is this fact: The world presents itself to us, and we take in the world. We don't see the seams, the cracks, and the imperfections.

We haven't missed a thing.

To the Lighthouse; again.

Lily Briscoe is painting on the lawn . . .

TO THE LIGHTHOUSE

VIRGINIA WOOLF

This painting of hers, with its abstractions, is Woolf's central metaphor for the act of creation in general—a writer or poet or composer's reconstruction of this slippery world of ours. More specifically, the painting is a proxy for the book *To the Lighthouse* by Virginia Woolf.

How does Lily Briscoe's painting reproduce the scene? Mrs. Ramsay, James, the house, the window?

> *But the picture was not of them, she said. Or not in his sense. There are other senses too in which one might reverence them. By a shadow here and a light there, for instance. Her tribute took that form if, as she vaguely supposed, a picture must be a tribute. A mother and child might be reduced to a shadow without irreverence.*

ES POUR LA DÉ

ÉMERAU

SÉRIE
P

ME CHROME

DECORATION AR

FRANC & C\ie

MINE ORAN

DECORATION AR

FRANC & C\ie—P

C D'ARG

BONATE DE PU

er white mi

nserweiss

NC & C\ie—

QUE DE GARA

ORDINAIRE

Madder lake

Krapplack

EFRANC—PA

SIENNE

Burnt Sien

di Sienna g

EFRANC—

EU DE CO

MINATE DE CO

Cobalt blue

Cobaltblau

FRANC—P

We reduce.

Writers reduce when they write, and readers reduce when they read. The brain itself is built to reduce, replace, emblemize . . . Verisimilitude is not only a false idol, but also an unattainable goal. So we reduce. And it is not without reverence that we reduce. This is how we apprehend our world. This is what humans do.

Picturing stories is making reductions. Through reduction, we create meaning.

These reductions are the world as we see it—they are what we see when we read, and they are what we see when we read the world.

They are what reading looks like (if it looks like anything at all).

***

Lily painting:

> *And she lost consciousness of outer things, and her name and her personality and her appearance, and whether Mr. Carmichael was there or not, her mind kept throwing up from its depths, scenes, and names, and sayings, and memories and ideas, like a fountain spurting over that glaring, hideously difficult white space . . . But this is one way of knowing people, she thought: to know the outline, not the detail.*

The outline. Not the detail.

There it was, her picture. Yes, with all its greens and blues, its lines running up and across, its attempt at something . . . She looked at the steps; they were empty; she looked at her canvas; it was blurred.

***

It was blurred.

***

Acknowledgments

I am grateful to many people, chief among these: Lexy Bloom, Jeff Alexander, Peter Terzian, Anne Messitte, Ben Shykind, Glenn Kurtz, Jenny Pouech, Sonny Mehta, Bridget Carey, Michael Silverberg, Dan Cantor, Peter Pitzele, Russell Perreault, Claudia Martinez, Tom Pold, Dan Frank, Barbara Richard, Roz Parr, Paige Smith, Megan Wilson, Carol Carson, Tony Chirico, Kate Runde, Stephen McNabb, Jaime De Pablos, LuAnn Walther, Quinn O'Neill, Mike Jones, everyone at Vintage Books, Jennifer Olsen, Pablo Delcan, Oliver Munday, Cardon Webb, David Wike, Max Fenton, Arthur Danto, Wallace Gray; my first and best audience: Judy Mendelsund and Lisa Mendelsund, and, always, Karla.

Finally: Thanks to the book cover designers—that loosely federated body of artists, publishing subalterns, and perpetual underclass. I'm proud to be one of your membership.

Permissions

Saint Isaac's Cathedral in St. Petersburg © Alinari Archives/The Image Works; *Portrait of a Lady* by Franz Xaver Winterhalter/ Private Collection/Photo © Christie's Images/The Bridgeman Art Library; *Portrait of an Unknown Woman, 1883* by Ivan Nikolae-vich Kramskoy; Greta Garbo as Anna Karenina © SV Bilder-dienst/DIZ Muenchen/The Image Works; Greta Garbo by George Hurrell; Movie star © Ronald Grant Archive/Mary Evans/The Image Works; Man reading icon made by Freepik from Flaticon .com; Dead chicken © mhatzapa/Shutterstock; Gerry Mulligan © Bob Willoughby/Redferns/Getty Images; Carey Mulligan © Tom Belcher/Capital Pictures/Retna Ltd.; A Hubble Space Telescope image of the typical globular cluster Messier 80/NASA; Mona Lisa Paint-by-Numbers courtesy of Don Brand (Mobii); Nabokov Metamorphosis notes © Vladimir Nabokov, courtesy of the Vlad-imir Nabokov Archive at the Berg Collection, New York Public Library, used by permission of The Wylie Agency LLC; Joyce drawing courtesy of the Charles Deering McCormick Library of Special Collections, Northwestern University; Drawing of Three Women Boarding a Streetcar While Two Men Watch by William Faulkner, used by permission of W. W. Norton & Company, Inc.; Lion Tamer by Gibson & Co. courtesy the Library of Congress; Ro-land Barthes © Ulf Andersen/Getty Images; Nabokov novel map © Vladimir Nabokov, courtesy of the Vladimir Nabokov Archive at the Berg Collection, New York Public Library, used by permission of The Wylie Agency LLC; *The Hobbit* © The J R R Tolkien Es-tate Limited 1937, 1965. Reprinted by permission of HarperCollins Publisher Ltd; William Wordsworth by Edwin Edwards courtesy of The British Library; scene from *Last Year at Marienbad*, photo: The Kobal Collection at Art Resource, NY; *The Ecstasy of St. Te-resa* by Gian Lorenzo Bernini courtesy of Alinari/Art Resource, NY; Pipe by Magritte © VOOK/Shutterstock; Achilles by Ernest Hester © Panagiotis Karapanagiotis/Alamy; Pentagon courtesy of the Library of Congress; Mercury Comet courtesy of Ford Images

"Levin gazed at the portrait, which stood out from the frame in the brilliant light thrown on it, and he could not tear himself away from it . . . It was not a picture, but a living, charming woman, with black curling hair, with bare arms and shoulders, with a pensive smile on the lips, covered with soft down; triumphantly and softly she looked at him with eyes that baffled him. She was not living only because she was more beautiful than a living woman can be."

—*Anna Karenina*